A DISTURBANCE IN THE FARCE

PUKE: THE FINAL CHAPTER, VOLUME 1

Mark Sieve

CIC Productions
Minneapolis, Minnesota

Copyright© 2019 Mark Sieve

ISBN 978-1-7333191-0-2 (softcover)

ISBN 978-1-7333191-1-9 (ebook)

Cover photo: Lonn Simmons
Cover design: Elder Carson
Editor: Marly Cornell

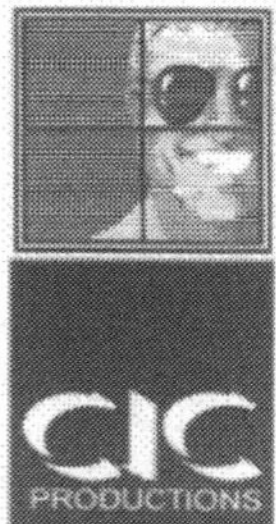

CIC Productions
4519 17th Avenue South
Minneapolis, Minnesota 55407
www.pukeandsnot.com

CONTENTS

FOREWORD

When I met Mark Sieve, I was twenty-three, and he was thirty-four. He had an apartment with no roommates. It was 1977, and we were in a play together, a comedy at a community theater. I was God, who in this case was a Puerto Rican steam bath attendant. Mark was the lead, dressed only in a towel in a steam bath that was purgatory. I have never intentionally been on stage since that show (not because of some "I've-played-God-where-do-you-go-from-there?" instinct, but because I was a terrible actor). But Mark and I have been good friends, colleagues, and confidantes for more than four decades since my retirement from the stage.

I was with him at the hospital when his son was born; I took him to the hospital when his father was dying. We have shared box seats at ball games, condos on guy getaways, bowling balls, golf clubs, cars, and more. (I am generous when I say "shared," as his stuff is always so much nicer than mine.)

The Minnesota theater scene is a robust one, with more than 400 theaters and unparalleled quality. It is well funded, well attended, and city and state leaders boast about it as an indication of the quality of life, on par with walleye fishing.

Mark Sieve has probably been seen by more people, has collected more money in beer steins, and has more devoted fans than any actor I have known in Mill City. Yet he is relatively unknown to most stage connoisseurs.

At the Mixed Blood Theatre, where I was even when I was God, Mark has been involved with many productions and operations—as an actor, director, board member, and even an emcee (in front of 3,000 American Express financial advisors in Nashville).

Mixed Blood Theatre is about cultural collisions that often manifest themselves in race—people with differences coming together and being better off for having convened. For an organization eschewing tokenism, Mark has been Mixed Blood's "white guy," blending unrecognized privilege with honesty and empathy even when his characters do villainous and heinous things. From smarmy real estate salesman to callous DMV bureaucrat to competitive antebellum slave owner to liberal New York aristocrat to used car salesman to manipulative Major League executive, Mark has, through poise, talent, and charm, grounded scurrilous characters in a foundation of historical and societal context seasoned with sympathy.

Mark is a consummate actor, skilled in comedy and drama,

contemporary and historical plays, realism, and stylized absurdism. Yet for the entire time I have known him, he has supported a family and middle class lifestyle based on dollars earned two days a week for five months a year doing a thirty-minute mock-Shakespeare show outdoors, in tights, with swords, as a character named Puke.

As a quick aside, who am I to comment on his alter ego's name, Puke, when I run a joint called Mixed Blood?

There is a third part of that trifecta for me: a famous indie music store in Minneapolis called The Electric Fetus. I have always contended that there is a cosmic force such that if any of those three—The Puke and Snot Show, Mixed Blood Theatre, or The Electric Fetus—ceased to operate, all three would have to crumble.

Our love of sports has bonded us and I was enamored that Mark had been drafted by Billy Martin and the Twins while playing college baseball. (My life goal was to either be a veterinarian or a shortstop for the Twins, and I run a theater in a 130-year-old firehouse.)

Mixed Blood has produced plays about baseball, football, basketball, soccer, bowling, golf, boxing, and pro wrestling, and Mark has been involved with many. The first show he directed was about Muhammad Ali, one that we'd written in six weeks after Ali beat Spinks to regain his championship belt. By this time Mark was thirty-five and a Minneapolis middle school teacher.

After opening, one of the cast members asked if Mark had ever directed professionally before. I'd forgotten to ask. But the cast was great (our company plus a big Bubba to play Jerry Quarry); the process was solid, the time limited, and the show was a hit. Our course was charted.

Mixed Blood became scouting camp for Puke and Snot (several actors became P&S "clones") and Mark became a theatrical fixture at Mixed Blood and remains one to this day, more than four decades later. Also a dear, dear friend. For all of his on-stage overblown pomposity, bravado, and hyperbole, Mark Sieve is a tender human. From weddings to funerals to relationship crises to ill health to financial maelstroms to car troubles to career confusion, Mark and I have traversed life as mutual advisors (although I can't remember once when we took each other's advice, but we are both active listeners).

In our many years as playmates, Mark Sieve and I have probably played golf or gone bowling 100 times. My guess is that his record is 98–2. Those two were not days I won, but rather I beat him on one hole one day and won one game of bowling on a Sunday morning, days after his knee had been replaced.

His competitive spirit outshines any pity he may muster, but his generosity knows no bounds. On a milestone birthday, I got a new set of golf clubs from Mark to replace the 1972 Pings I was using. I used to have *one* season ticket to the Vikings, so while I couldn't take him to games, we watched the away games together at my home. One day he showed up with a new flat-screen TV to replace the giant tube 19-incher of my mom's that I'd been using.

"I couldn't even read the jersey numbers!" he remarked. That is the embodiment of Mark. He recognizes a problem and solves it with grace, kindness, and thoughtfulness.

Aside #2. I have an odd affinity for symmetrical numbers. My mother was born in '22, graduated from the University of Minnesota in '44, and died in '99 at the age of 77. I have three cars: an '88, '99, and '11. I founded The Mixed Blood Theatre on 2/2 at the age of 22 and have now run it for 44 years, which makes me 66 and the father of a 33-year old daughter who was born when I was 33.

My favorite holidays are New Year's Day, Groundhog Day, Cinco de Mayo, and Armistice Day because they're 1/1, 2/2, 5/5, and 11/11. So in '77 when I learned that Mark Sieve's birthday was 12/12, I knew we'd be friends for life.

We took a show to New York for a seven-week Off-Broadway run in 2009. Mark got rave reviews, as did the show. After three weeks, he left the show to be Puke in Colorado. Mark is a versatile actor, but in his soul, he is and always will be Puke. His partner of thirty-four years, Joe Kudla, died on a Monday and there was a new Snot on stage by Saturday. "That's one way to freshen up an act," I quipped.

But I knew that day that Puke and Snot was not a frivolous gimmick Mark concocted to collect some coins, but that he valued the art and science of the writing and performance of comedy in general and was intent on perfecting it with his own niche in the comedy universe.

My esteem for him, already at a zenith, grew exponentially as his heart and mind melded and melted in loss and possibility. The theater needs more Mark Sieves, and I and Mixed Blood have been the beneficiary of his treasures and gifts.

—Jack Reuler, founder and artistic director,
Mixed Blood Theatre Company
Minneapolis, Minnesota

FIRSTLY

I shouldn't even be here. I was five seconds from extinction on a breezy, summer afternoon in 1959. On her way back to the family farm that day, Mom drove by the fresh and dusty ruins of the new bowling alley that until five minutes before had been standing proudly with four walls and half the rafters in place and me as one of the unskilled hired hands.

From her car she saw my red Schwinn bike lying next to crumbled concrete and splintered rafters. She pulled over, leaped out, and screamed my name as she threw aside broken boards, chunks of plaster, and rock.

Another driver stopped, hearing her yell, "My son's under here! Help me!"

They both resumed a frantic search for my remains. The evidence pointed to me being buried somewhere deep beneath the twisted wreckage of Harlan's Lanes/Under Construction.

Within minutes, another driver pulled up and asked what they were doing. They yelled at him to help them dig for me, and he laughed. "I just saw him on the street downtown with Harlan. They were heading into Adrian's."

Mom started crying, half from relief and half in anger that her eldest son would fake his own death. Meanwhile, oblivious to the raw drama unfolding a half-mile away at Harlan's Lanes/Under Demolition, I left Adrian Shoemaker's Insurance ("Forget my exclusions, let's talk about your limitations!") to grab a Coke at my parent's café across the street.

When I walked in, Vivian the waitress chirped, "You better get home, your mom thinks you're dead."

Vivian was a desperately jolly woman who lived the next farm down from us and had six daughters. Her favorite joke whenever Mom sent her to the bakery for fresh rolls and hamburger buns for the café was, "Okay, I'm going to get "bred." *Hahahahaha*." None of us ever thought that line was amusing.

Holy shit. Mom must have seen Harlan's wreckage! My bike. Damn! I beelined out the front door of the Grill Café, flagged down Harlan, and told him to get me home fast.

Harlan was the unfortunate owner of the doomed bowling alley. When he stepped around the lone standing wall after the enormous rumbling crashing noise on the other side and saw the other three walls and the rafters and supports all lying in a dusty heap, Harlan's first words were "Oh my gosh! What did you do?

Golly! Holy smokes! Get in the car, we have to see Adrian about the insurance right now!" (Harlan was a devout Christian man, and this is about as profane as he would ever get.)

I was lying on my face in the rocks and dirt and broken boards ten feet from the ruins, where I had landed after leaping Spidey-like from the top of the wall. I saw the rafters of the unfinished roof slowly collapsing toward me like falling dominoes while I was standing with my hammer in the very center of the roof, nailing those same rafters together.

I had felt the breeze suddenly gust, heard an ominous cracking sound, and something in my farm-boy sense of self-preservation made me look up and see Approaching Death. I turned, took four fast hops along two rafters, reached the wall, and jumped, landing and rolling and covering my head with my arms as concrete blocks and splintered lumber fell around me.

Harlan didn't ask if I was hurt. I wasn't, but he could have asked.

Harlan and I were connected through his older, abandoned six-lane bowling alley downtown, where I had worked as a pin setter for seven cents a line for a couple of years along with some of my high school friends. On a league bowling night, we could make two or three bucks in a three-hour shift racking pins and sitting on a shelf behind them where we made ourselves small to avoid getting hit by flying wooden pins as the big boys from the VFW Club rolled sixteen-pounders down the middle.

Now Harlan was paying me two bucks an hour to risk my life once again to help him build his new emporium. Two bucks an hour wasn't bad in 1959 for a small-town kid with no car and no social life.

He dropped me at the farm, I walked into the kitchen where Mom saw me and burst into fresh tears. I told her I was sorry I hadn't thought to call her and tell her what happened, but that Harlan was panicking about his insurance and I had to go with him. It was just fate that she drove by immediately after we left.

The survivor of the Harlan's Lanes disaster and his relieved rescuer.

Harlan had hired a relative from the Twin Cities to bring a crew to our little central Minnesota burg to lay the foundation and build the framework for his new alleys. I saw immediately that Harlan's cousin and his crew were a little different. They started passing around a bottle at 10:00 in the morning and were still going at it when we quit at 6:00 p.m. Before this, I had never heard pirate shanties sung on a construction site in Minnesota.

I'm not now and have never been a litigious man, but it occurred to me at the time: had I been hurt or banged up in any way in the collapse, a first-year law student could probably have negotiated a strong settlement from Adrian's insurance company. The wind didn't knock down Harlan's Lanes. Captain Morgan and his drunken pirates did.

So I shouldn't be here. I got lucky. Good luck has been a steady and consistent theme in my life.

As a golfing buddy said to me after my third hole in one dropped into the cup a couple of years ago, "Have you checked to make sure you don't have a rabbit's foot up your butt?"

Here I am, at the same age my dad was when he died, looking back on the odd little twists and turns of providence that marked my survival to this ripe old age of I-don't-want-to-talk-about-it-right-now-I'm-in-denial. I could easily have earned my wings that time in British Columbia when my motorcycle drifted over the center line into the path of an eighteen-wheeler as I admired the sunset over the coastal mountains.

I could have climbed the golden staircase at the age of six when I turned around from the water fountain on the corner in my little southern Minnesota town, started across the street to catch up with my good friend Duke, and woke up a few minutes later with a stranger carrying me into my parent's café after he ran over me with his Studebaker.

I could have hung up my hat from prostate cancer like my dad, but they caught it in time and now I'm the punch line for one of the oldest jokes in the history of comedy:

DOCTOR: I've got good news and bad news.

ME: Okay, what's the good news?

DOCTOR: We saved your prostate.

ME: That's great. What's the bad news?

DOCTOR: It's in that jar on the shelf.

Or the heart attacks, both of them, the first one in '96 when I whined about a radiating pain up and down my left arm during a round of golf with my usual foursome. An older and wiser friend told me to get my butt to a hospital forthwith. I didn't, I was only fifty-four. And even though both my mom and my dad had open heart surgeries and my brother Mike had bypass surgery at the age of forty-three, and I knew my family manufactured cholesterol at nearly the same rate Skippy made peanut butter, I was way too young for heart trouble. But I found myself on the sofa in my downtown office the next afternoon trying to take a nap before a meeting. Just before I drifted off, I opened my eyes wide and, with chilling clarity, suddenly realized that I *never* took naps in the office.

I called my wife, Jan, and told her I was going to drive over to Methodist Hospital and get checked out. I did. After taking my history and some blood, three doctors put their heads together and whispered at each other for a few minutes. When they broke up their little meeting, they told me they were keeping me overnight for observation.

I called Jan and asked her to bring me some fresh underwear. The next morning at 5:00 a.m., a small committee in gowns and hospital uniforms woke me and way-too-cheerfully informed me that I had experienced a "small" heart attack, and they wanted to take me upstairs for an angiogram to find the blockage.

This was unexpected news before breakfast. They gave me a valium, and a few minutes later I was lying in the OR with a stupid grin on my face, watching the TV monitors as a doctor shot ink into my arteries.

I saw the exact spot on my heart where the ink stopped flowing for a moment, then appeared again in a tiny trickle a half inch down the artery. I heard him chuckle happily, "There it is! This one will be easy, we'll do it with a wire, just stay comfortable and I'll get the surgeon in here in a few minutes."

Wait. What? You're not the surgeon? What are you doing shooting ink around my heart?

But I knew what "do it with a wire" meant. My brother Mike's arterial blockage was in an inconvenient place on his heart, and they had to open him up like a Thanksgiving turkey. I was—once again—lucky.

Angioplasty is a piece o' cake. You'll have more discomfort getting your teeth cleaned than you will getting an artery reamed out.

Fast forward ten years. I'm unloading some audio/video equipment from my Jeep into a storage facility on a lovely spring day, and I notice I'm sweating and feeling nauseous. *Weird, I'm not even working that hard and the building is air-conditioned. Hmm. . .* the same chilling clarity, *something's wrong here.*

I yelled at a guy in another locker to close up mine, I had to get out of there. I jumped in the Jeep, took a right turn out of the building, and found myself in the left-turn lane at a red light, waiting for a train to clear the crossing. I suddenly knew I needed to move. I couldn't wait. I considered running the light and trying to beat the train, but I held back. When it finally cleared, I floored it for home, a couple of miles away. But within twenty blocks, I knew I had to stop, get out, and get help.

I saw the old fire station at the corner of 42nd and Cedar, so I parked the Jeep on the street, and walked—gingerly and slowly—to the side door of the fire station, completely forgetting that the building hadn't been a fire station for five years. I opened the door and was met with a concrete floor full of cubicles, with people at desks on their phones and computers. "Excuse me, you guys are all EMTs, right?" I asked hopefully.

"No, we're architects," said the guy at the desk closest to me.

"Well, somebody call an ambulance, I think I'm having a heart attack, and I don't want to die here in your office."

A dozen people instantly grabbed their phones and dialed 911, I sat down on the floor and leaned against the wall, trying to locate a radiating pain or some chest pressure or anything that would tell me how long I might have to live. Within a couple of minutes I heard the sirens, the Twin Cities being the kind of forward-looking metro area where you're never more than three minutes from medical help.

The first responders came hustling into the former-fire-station-now-goddam-architectural-firm, peeled back my shirt, slapped some sensors on my chest, put me on a stretcher, and got me out of there into the ambulance. Soon we were barreling toward Hennepin County Medical Center in downtown Minneapolis where a half dozen people in green scrubs hustled me out and tore off my clothes. A nurse said, "You're in luck, the head of Surgery is in today, and he's going to take care of you."

They rolled me in and saved my life.

Once again, born under a lucky star.

That ride to the hospital was memorable for another reason. While I was sitting on the floor of the old fire station waiting for help, I called my son Pete in his car and told him an ambulance was on its way and to meet us at Methodist Hospital. In the ambulance I asked if that's where they were taking me and somebody said, "No, we don't have time for that, we're taking you to Hennepin County Medical Center, it's closer."

I started to call Pete to tell him the plan had changed, but a nurse grabbed my phone and said, "Do you mind? We're trying to save your life."

I asked her to call Pete and tell him the plan had changed. She did, and when Pete got a call from Dad's phone, he picked it up to hear a woman's voice with a siren in the background and immediately thought Dad was a goner. Freaked the boy out.

I could have shuffled off this mortal coil a hundred different ways in the short five years we lived on the farm while I was in high school. Small family farms are extremely dangerous places, especially for children.

My dad once told me the reason so many German Catholic farm families in Minnesota had more than six kids was that it was always assumed that you'd lose one or two of them along the way in some horrific accident like a stock tank drowning, a power takeoff mangling, a haymow suffocation, a tractor rollover, a mower amputation, a silage collapse, a pitchfork stabbing, or just being trampled by a bull or eaten by pigs. And a farm needs workers, lots of them. My dad had five brothers and three sisters, and none of them stayed in school beyond the eighth grade.

In the early years of the twentieth century, eight grades was more than enough education to learn how to read and write and do your numbers. Kids were usually physically developed enough at fourteen to start regular shifts in the barn and in the fields.

I have cousins in southern Minnesota who had twelve and thirteen children. They were good rhythm-method-practicing Catholics all, but it was even more about economics. They were simply ensuring there would never be a labor shortage on their farm.

So I'm playing with house money, as my good friend the ace gambler and second Snot, John Gamoke, would tell me. I survived long enough to write another book.

And right there you have a classic illustration of your good news and bad news.

↾⇀

"I grow old, I grow old
 I shall wear the bottoms of my trousers rolled."
                    —T. S. Eliot, "The Love Song of J. Alfred Prufrock"

In late October of 2016, John and I had just finished a show on the Royal Fox Stage in Crownsville, Maryland, and were sweatily recovering at the merchandise cart behind the audience, signing CDs, and chatting with patrons. A group of seven or eight college kids walked by and one of them, a guy in a tank top, tattoos, and a few prominent piercings, recognized us, stopped, and said, "You guys are *hilarious*." Before we could thank him, he finished his thought. "You're older than fuck, but you're *hilarious*."

Stifling the urge to reply with a professional killer put-down, I smiled grimly and said, "Thanks. Appreciate it."

It was, after all, a compliment. John and I nodded in admiration. The best moments bubble up from the Wellspring of Truth.

I am definitely older than fuck. John is just older than shit. If I were to be truthful—and we like that in our memoirists, don't we?—there was a brief moment with the Tattooed Wiseass when I wished I had the presence of mind of an astute musician friend when he faced a similar circumstance. And he's much younger than I.

He said, "Some school kids walked by me today and one said, 'Hi Dad,' and they all laughed and I laughed too, but with a laugh that said, *I will destroy you and everything you love, leaving only a brittle husk with vacant eyes emptied by horrors unimaginable.*"

That's delicious; and he did it with a laugh. Jeremy Messersmith has a way with words even when he doesn't use them.

Even so, moments like that are becoming less jarring as the years whiz by and the gray hairs keep finding new places on my body to sprout and spread. I'm getting so hairy I need a shampoo called Head and Shoulders and Back and Chest and Butt and Legs. It's not my joke, but it's my truth.

Joe and I began this Puke and Snot journey when I was thirty-one and he was twenty-three. Now in the summer of 2019, the show is lurching along with more jokes about age and its accompanying difficulties: bad knees, constipation, lost prostates, digestion, forgetfulness, hearing problems, ED.

With Joe gone and John recently retired, the younger but still extremely Snot-like Scott Jorgenson and I are adapting the show to the realities of the aging process.

PUKE   You know the best thing about being the oldest act at a Renaissance festival?

SNOT   What?

PUKE   No peer pressure.

SNOT   You HAVE been at this awhile, haven't you . . .

PUKE   Yes. I always thought growing old would take longer. It's been a long time on this stage, sometimes it's almost depressing. One time I even threatened to jump off a cliff.

SNOT   Did you?

PUKE   No, it was just a bluff.

SNOT   Quit worrying. People overcome adversity all the time. Look at Beethoven. They told him he was deaf, but did he listen?

PUKE   [REFLECTIVE] I'm kind of like this ship, floating atop a deep unfathomable darkness, full of terrifying things.

SNOT   Well, I was going to say "old and wooden," but sure. What are you going to do when this festival's over?

PUKE   I want to buy some land.

SNOT   That's asking for a lot.

PUKE   At my age, a man needs some security. You're too young
         to know what I'm talking about.

SNOT   I'm older than you think. Yesterday I found my first gray
         pubic hair.

PUKE   That must have been exciting.

SNOT   Not as exciting as it was for the other people on the bus.

All personal challenges related to age are fair game for self-mockery, and they all get a tryout in rehearsal before the final cuts are made. We have yet to come up with a joke as perfect as the one George Burns created when an interviewer asked him what having sex was like at the age of one hundred: "It's like shooting pool with a rope."

In the unlikely event I ever reach triple digits, there is no chance I'll ever come up with an old guy joke better than that.

In Toronto in the early eighties with Penn and Teller, walking over to an Elvis Costello concert one night at the hockey arena, Penn tried to convince Joe and me to change our stage names to something that better represented our actual personas. Penn was aware that Joe was deaf in one ear; and without my glasses, I am legally blind.

PENN   The names Puke and Snot say nothing about who you
         really are. You should call yourselves Stump and Post.

JOE   Why?

PENN   It's perfect. He's blind as a stump, and you're deaf as a
        post.

ME   We'll think about it.

Many years later, Penn's words return like the ghost of
Hamlet's father to haunt my ramparts. My eyesight hasn't improved,
and I occasionally use hearing aids. I am now in Stump-AND-Post
territory. Penn always was a wise and prescient bastard.

But of course growing older with a few impediments is far
preferable to the alternative. No complaining here, just good-natured
anxiety and nervous laughter.

A curious dynamic has repeated itself at least a half-dozen
times in the years since Joe died. The first time it happened, I was
on a rental car bus in Denver, sitting near a threesome of women
who were obviously traveling together. As they chatted and I
scrolled through messages on my cell, one of them looked at me and
blurted, "Hey! You're one of those Renaissance guys, aren't you?"

"I could be," I said.

"No, you definitely are," she continued, "I've seen your show.
One of you died. Which one?"

Short pause while I mentally shuffled through my options. I
settled on, "I'm pretty sure it was him."

"Oh! NO! You know what I mean!"

The other two looked slightly uncomfortable, perhaps thinking
I was offended.

I said, "Are you asking, was it Puke or Snot who died?"

"Yes, which one?"

"It was the shorter one."

She gave up without giving me the chuckle I thought I deserved. But I retained my professional wise-ass title. In the months and years since, I have developed a short list of better answers to that inevitable question. And I love it when it happens.

Two years ago at the Minnesota Renaissance Festival, I was standing in our merchandise shop, watching two well-dressed women looking at the Puke & Snot media collection. One of them pointed to a CD with Joe and me on the cover and said, "Both of them died, you know."

The other one looked at me. Brief pause. "No, I don't think so."

"Yes, both of them. The two guys doing the show now are both replacements. I read it somewhere."

I quietly slipped out of the shop, leaving them to sort it out.

The fact remains, pun intended, not being dead yet is universally funny. In *Monty Python and the Holy Grail*, the corpse collector and the peasant dropping a dead relative off at the cart who "isn't quite dead yet" have one of the funniest scenes in the movie.

Google "bring out your dead" and giggle darkly. The brilliance of that scene lies in the absolute certainty we feel that those were the exact conditions in England during the Plague Years. The mud, the filth, the death, and quite likely, the exquisitely morbid jokes.

Now that we're off to a cheery start, let's settle in and take a little saunter down memory lane—my memory, mate, not yours—to one of my first onstage adventures, where I played, naturally, a corpse.

1

DON'T KISS ME, I'M DEAD

When I stepped onstage at Long Prairie High School in my first dramatic role at the age of sixteen under a bank of lights in front of an audience of family, friends, and neighbors, no part of the experience had anything to do with art. Galloping adolescent hormones and the intriguing discovery that high school girls liked dressing up and doing plays drove my decision to audition for the spring production.

A chance to hang with the ladies after school? Of course! It didn't hurt that my best friend, Larry, the hard-nosed fullback on our football team, had the same idea. Who would question our choice to dabble in the performing arts if he were involved? Genius.

I was yet unaware of Samuel Johnson's note to his friend and actor, David Garrick, "I'll come no more behind your scenes, David, for the silk stockings and white bosoms of your actresses do make my genitals to quiver." Instinctively, Larry and I were fearlessly, and with far less trepidation, treading the same ground as Mr. Johnson many generations earlier.

To my surprise I was cast as the city dad in *January Thaw*, a "farm life vs. city life" play filled with standard gags about an urban family adapting to new lives on the farm. The play required actual baby pigs and chickens onstage. Plenty of manure jokes.

I had the lead and some of the best lines. Getting laughs from the generous audiences of parents and friends was like the *Simpson's* episode when Barney guzzled his first beer with Homer: "Where has this been all my life?"

I hadn't been in a play since a traumatic grade school appearance as one of the three kings in the Christmas pageant: the long terrifying entrance from the back of the classroom, down the long aisle to the stage, all eyes on me as I kept tripping on my robe while I sang my solo, "Myrrh is mine, its bitter perfume . . ." And as I handed her my gift, Mary threw up in the manger. More than enough to permanently drive a boy away from the theater.

Over many years of watching late-night television, we've all seen and heard the stars tell their backstage stories. Tales of missed entrances, falling sets, disappearing props, inebriated King Lears, guns that fail to fire, actors falling into the front row during blackouts, unforeseen disasters that at the moment may have seemed career-ending, but in the fullness of time are just amusing.

Richard Harris, Peter O'Toole, and Richard Burton were three brilliant actors and friends, who were nearly as famous for their notorious drinking episodes, often while they were performing. Burton once told Johnny Carson that he couldn't remember any of his movies, he was drunk the whole time he was filming them.

Harris used to tell the story of the night he and O'Toole were doing a play together in London's West End. They had a twenty-minute window of time in the play when neither one of them was onstage, so every night they'd zip across the street to a pub and knock down a couple of beers, all the while watching the clock to make sure they were back for their next entrance.

But one night they got into an animated discussion and lost track of time. Suddenly the stage manager came running into the pub yelling, "Harris! O'Toole! For God's sake, you're on! The play has stopped, and they're waiting for you!"

They leaped up (finished their beers of course), ran out into the street, dodged a taxi and a truck, hurtled backstage, and as Harris, who was on before O'Toole, ran out onstage, he tripped over a wire and went sprawling on his belly, sliding across the stage until his head and upper torso were hanging off the front in the lap of an older woman. "Good God!" she screamed, "You're drunk!"

Calmly smiling, Harris said, "Madam, if you think I'm drunk, wait'll you see the Duke of Gloucester."

Nearly fifty years of professional theater has supplied me with more than my share of tales, some of which you will encounter if you continue reading beyond this page. You've been warned.

But this high school drama scene was all new to me, the

memorization, rehearsals, the sets and props, the costumes, the makeup. It seemed complicated, with lots of moving parts. And since no one else in the cast had any theater experience, it was communal discovery at every step, so no one felt out of his depth. Our director, Don Corcoran, a gentle and infinitely patient teacher, made it fun. He let us freely explore the process to come up with our own versions of these one-dimensional characters.

First dramatic role, sporting the tallest crew cut in Todd County, 1959.

It was a grand time and we all dove right in. I made a quick costume change one night, running onstage to start the scene and, before I could say my first line, chuckles and laughs bubbled up from the crowd.

Thought I: *You're good at this acting thing—you're funny before you even say a word.*

Seeing Larry staring at me, I glanced down and saw that in the frenzy of the quick change backstage, I had tucked my pantlegs into my socks, my fly was open, and I was now standing center stage making an unintended fashion statement. If I'd have known what a "dresser" was—besides the place in my bedroom where I stashed my socks and underwear—I'd have asked for one the next day.

By the time the senior play rolled around the following year, I saw myself as a veteran lead actor. I went to auditions cocky and convinced I'd play the meaty male lead as the inspector in the murder mystery *Meet a Body*.

Instead I was cast as the unsympathetic rich guy who gets killed and spends most the rest of the play in an open coffin. I was to be The Body.

The good news: I got the title role. The bad news: I died at the end of act one. Other than remaining, literally, deathly still for the entirety of Act Two, my work was essentially done by intermission. I shrugged off my disappointment and decided to make this the most intriguing and memorable corpse anybody in that little town had ever encountered.

Rehearsals chugged along. By opening night I was comfortable in the role, and my ego was at peace with my limited stage time. My coffin was actually fairly cozy, with a clean and firm pillow, and I had worked on my shallow breathing to keep the corpse quite motionless and believably dead.

At one point in the second act, my "wife," who was being played by a classmate I barely knew, is overcome with emotion and leans into the open casket to plant a farewell kiss on the cold remains of her beloved. According to Director Don, it was to be a simple, mimed kiss that didn't actually make contact, an agreeable solution to my understandable reluctance at being involved in anything resembling necrophilia.

My grieving wife was to be positioned upstage between the deceased and the audience. They couldn't see the kiss, so there was thankfully no need for anything physical.

But on opening night, the scene went grotesquely awry. My distraught wife, pumped up by a live audience and emitting howling, Shakespearean grief (far more than any of us had seen at any rehearsal), leaned over the casket and gave me a huge, open-mouthed lip-lock that seemed to go on for minutes.

Her breath was broccoli-esque. I couldn't breathe. Worse, I couldn't protest without breaking character and coming back to life. So I let her have her way with me. My disgust was palpable, but my self-control and stony cadaver-like acceptance was the best acting I'd done in two years.

I learned something important about the theater that night—about the need to get to know your fellow actors, bond with them in a common purpose, and create a minimal level of trust. If things get weird, at least you'll have established a relationship with the person who's trying to stick her tongue down your throat.

If I could time machine myself back to that night, knowing what I know now about improvisation, I would lurch upright in the coffin and scream, "It's ALIVE!," then stalk off the stage like Frankenstein's monster and let the chips fall where they may. That little town on the Minnesota prairie would still be talking about it.

2

MR. BOJANGLES WOULD

LIKE A WORD WITH YOU

My usual smartass thought, before I mentally punch myself in the head and respond civilly to the question, "Why did you become an actor?," is usually something like "It was easier than learning the piano." Truthfully, and in my defense, I became an actor because I was left unsupervised.

I was drawn to the theater by the attention you get when the theater is dark and you're onstage in a bright light, sometimes alone, sinking or swimming. It feels risky every night, and it gets your heart rate up no matter how comfortable you are with a role. Is it a similar feeling experienced by cliff divers, parachutists, rock climbers? I'll never know; that shit scares the bejeesus out of me.

I'm sure it's also a pathetic desire to be that voice that all heads turn to hear, a way to say, night after night, "Here I am, I'm a person, I exist, I'm unique, I have worth, I'm good at this. Look at me, goddammit, I'm the One In The Spotlight!"

I was actually intimidated by pianos—and oboes, violins, clarinets, drums, and the people who could make music with them. Playing any instrument other than the cowbell, seemed like a skill reserved for savants. My parents paid the nuns at St. Mary's Catholic Elementary to teach me the piano. But with that mysterious penguin-like person perched next to me on the worn mahogany bench combined with the inevitable halitosis, I could never concentrate long enough to learn even the most basic exercises. (I walked out of *Batman Returns* the moment Danny DeVito appeared onscreen as the Penguin. Nightmares).

I got through one recital with a comically simple two-chord tune I can't remember. But meeting twice a week at the convent to continue the torture with Sister Mary Severeous leaning over my shoulder was a sentence I finally got commuted through youthful subterfuge: I remained stubbornly unwilling to distinguish the difference between A flat and B sharp. My parents finally had to admit they were wasting their money. To this day I am awestruck by anyone who can sit down and play anything more difficult than "Three Blind Mice."

One Minnesota winter, I was home from college for the holidays and Mom gave me twenty bucks to buy a neighbor's guitar for my younger brother, Jon, as a Christmas present.

I'd been listening to Bob Dylan, Joan Baez, and the Kingston

Trio on my high-tech, single-speaker Motorola turntable in my dorm room. I imagined morphing from a geeky crew-cut college kid into an actual troubadour, a dreamer of dreams, a singer of songs.

If Minnesota Bob Dylan could become famous with that gravelly voice, surely I could learn how to strum and sing well enough to impress the freshman girls at St. Benedict's. Again: art as a gateway drug to potential intimacy. (My therapist should hear about this, it could be important.)

Mom had no idea that learning the guitar had become an unspoken ambition of mine. And now my *brother* was going to get a guitar?

Holding the red Harmony six-string on my lap while its owner showed me a few chords that I could teach Jon, I envisioned a stage, a hushed crowd, a spotlight, a career! I had a personality, and I fully intended to use it one day.

I took the guitar home and quietly practiced in my room, discovering happily that most folk songs from the sixties required no more than three simple finger placements: D, A, G, and an occasional E minor for moody variety. Wow. Peter, Paul and Mary became legends with those three chords. (Yes, and some pretty tight harmonies, but one step at a time, and more about them later).

Brother Jon was excited when he saw his gift under the tree and went immediately to work learning the essentials of folk guitar. Jon had a good voice, he sang in the St. John's University Men's Chorus, and when I saw how quickly he picked up the basics of

Guitar 101/Three Chords to Carnegie Hall, I resolved to get my own instrument and engage this sibling rivalry immediately.

I did, spending way too much for a Martin six-string. Within a year, my brother and I were competent enough to create a song list of folk tunes from the era. Before long we were appearing locally at impromptu hootenannies, singing popular folk songs of the early sixties: *Shady Grove, If I Were A Carpenter, If I Had A Hammer,* lots of "*If I . . .*" songs whose historical framing we were clueless about, but "if we" had had the slightest self-awareness, we wouldn't have dared sing in public.

We sang slave songs, for God's sake. *Slave songs. The Ballad of John Henry, The Drinking Gourd,* songs that were rooted in black history, the Underground Railroad, the pain and suffering of generations of people we knew nothing about. We did our version of *Mr. Bojangles.* Yes we did. It makes my sphincter pucker just to think now about what never occurred to us at the time: two young white guys from central Minnesota blithely singing mournful Civil War era songs to equally blank white audiences.

John Belushi's classic destruction of the guitar on the staircase in *Animal House* years later was an inspired piece of comedy. Inspired by guys like us. We were that guy—times two—singing *"I gave my love a cherry that had no stone."*

We had not yet accepted Rule Three of The Golden Trinity of Being a Good Dude: 1) Wear a condom, 2) Don't drink and drive, and 3) Never, ever, ever play guitar at a party. By the time I graduated and started teaching, little brother and I had an extensive library of covers we could reliably trot out to anyone who'd listen.

My teaching career launched in the fall of 1964, and immediately I invited brother Jon to perform with me at student assemblies in the rural Minnesota high schools where I worked. Jon would arrive, we'd don matching blue denim shirts, and step out onstage to wow the kids.

We took our guitars with us everywhere. On a family train trip to New Mexico, we entertained the passengers in the dining car. On a ski trip to Austria, we got a good deal at Frau Lewisch's gasthof when she found out she was going to be lodging two "American folk singers." Yes, we took our guitars with us on a ski trip to Europe, the demand for American Civil War era slave songs peaking in Innsbruck at the time. We couldn't afford roadies, so we lugged our skis, boots, poles, guitars, and suitcases on and off the trains.

The Sieve Brother's American Folk Music and European Ski Tour reached Peak Stupidity the night we took two Swedish sister-skiers to dinner, went back to their place for a nightcap, sang a few folk songs to whet their appetite for romance, and brother Jon passed out on their carpet. Skiing, drinking, and singing—don't let the sneaky resort ads fool you; nobody gets lucky after a day like that.

Eventually I pursued a solo career and expanded my repertoire into the songs of John Prine, Gordon Lightfoot, Crosby Stills Nash and Young, and other artists whose work I admired. I began playing pizza parlors and beer joints for twenty-five bucks a night and all the blackberry brandy I could drink (a tip from a real professional, a former member of the New Christy Minstrels then touring as a solo act who I'd seen onstage one night: "Sip blackberry brandy, it's good for the vocal chords"). Complete bullshit. Alcohol actually dries out your vocal chords. But it made me feel like an artiste with a glass sitting next to me on a stool all night.

I paired up with Harry Maurer, a friend whose guitar and banjo work was strong and his enthusiasm infectious. At one point I worked with a standup bass player in an attempt to emulate the Smothers Brothers, and we booked some gigs in bars and pizza joints in Central Minnesota that required us to play three or four sets a night.

I figured out that unless I put a tight limit on the free blackberry brandy, I was repeating songs in set three I had sung much more lucidly in set one. But it was all good. My Kingston Trio crew cut was still fashionable, and I spent weekend evenings singing and playing other people's music.

The fact that I was working my craft in Minnesota farm country, light years from the urban centers where the next Dylans and Prines and Lightfoots were being discovered, never occurred to me. I had quit trying to figure out What Will Happen Next. Nobody knows that.

Life is a horrifying mystery. *"Sing a song, don't be long, thrill me to the marrow."*

3

12 STEPS? I CAN'T EVEN STAND UP

Social upheaval, civil unrest, race, and emerging issues of voting rights, justice for all, assassinations, the rise of the counterculture, the British music invasion, the Vietnam War—if you lived and worked in small-town Minnesota, the sixties actually happened on another planet.

Yes, you could hear the music, and the black-and-white images arriving daily on your fourteen-inch Curtis Mathes warned you that events unfolding in places like Da Nang and Haiphong and Memphis might someday disrupt and alter the idyllic lifestyle you enjoyed at the moment.

But if your college years were behind you, and you were a white guy like me with a degree from a prestigious private school, you were essentially farting through silk, as my old baseball coach at St. John's used to say. High school teaching jobs were plentiful. Schools all over the Upper Midwest were desperate for warm

31

bodies, and they weren't even that concerned if that body didn't come with a teaching license.

I taught for two years with a stoned Navy vet who was unlicensed but was still hired as a Social Studies teacher simply because the superintendent, a vet himself, thought the guy could at least maintain order in his classroom. If you wanted a teaching job, all you had to do was send in an application. You'd at least get an interview.

I was offered a job at my first meeting with a high school superintendent. The contract would pay me $4,700 for the school year to teach English and speech to five classes a day. I asked if there were any extra-curriculars I could take on to make a little extra money. By the time I left his office, I had agreed to direct three plays, supervise and direct the spring declamation contest, and coach middle school basketball and varsity baseball.

The sports jobs were easy. I had been a four-year letterman in college and a regular gym rat. But speech and theater? I'd be learning on the job. He saw on my resume that I had acted in a couple of productions in college, and deemed it enough to entrust me with the "Theater Program."

I added up the compensation package for agreeing to commit to a full year of afterschool activities, it came to a delightful $500. For everything. Still not bad, I was paying thirty dollars a month to rent a room at Elsie's house a few blocks from school.

Elsie was a personable older widow with an unfortunate case

of colitis. Her explosive gaseous episodes reverberated through the house at all hours, but for thirty dollars a month, it was something I could live with. Coaching and directing made my car and rent payments.

The head baseball coach contract paid me seventy-five dollars. I didn't find out till much later that the former coach, Ray, a revered long-tenured teacher and an experienced baseball man, had asked for a raise from fifty to seventy-five dollars, and the superintendent not only turned him down, but hired me at the same figure that Ray had requested. A petty and vindictive move.

I was a first-year teacher and had no clue how small-town politics and personal vendettas effected daily life and work in local public education. Ray was a good enough coach to have taken this tiny high school to the state tournament a few years before. I just hoped I could be good enough to be anonymous and let the kids play the game.

After sixteen straight years of schooling and guidance from nuns, lay people, monks, priests, and distinguished professors, I was finally free to begin making my own way, carving out my path to a long and successful career as a Teacher of Youth. It was energizing and freeing and altogether exciting. It wasn't more than a few months into it that I realized that many of my peers were full-time alcoholics.

🙞🙜

My own first beer was given to me at age sixteen by my father after a long, hot muggy day of baling hay on the family farm. I felt like Dad was solemnly handing me more than just a cold can of Grain Belt Premium, but a taciturn German-American son's admission that I was now a man. It tasted good.

Until that day, the only alcohol that had passed my lips was a few sips of Mogen David wine that Mom and Dad trotted out at Christmas—a thick, syrupy substance that neither I nor my brothers found particularly appealing.

I remember a slight bitterness with that first beer---whether it was the hops or just a simple metaphorical off-taste connected to my athletic training that said alcohol was forbidden, I don't know. But that beer, in the company of approving adult neighbors and friends, felt to me like much more than a simple, bracingly cold beverage awarded for a hard day's work—it felt like one more step out of childhood and into the world of men.

That beer was the last alcohol I drank until a couple of years later on a spring evening when I joined three college friends in a parked car in the autumn woods near a lake to share a bottle of gin one of them had sneaked into his dorm room. We passed it around, took deep, manly swigs, and wiped our mouths with the back of our sleeves like cowboys. We spoke profoundly about life, love, and philosophy, and kept our eyes open for passing adults who could blow the whistle on our illegal activity. The gin tasted terrible. I still can't drink it to this day.

College drinking—a universal rite of passage into adulthood—became a more conscious part of the extra-curriculum as we moved from freshman to sophomore years. The drinking age was twenty-one, and I wasn't, but just a few short miles away sat legendary watering holes like Brickey's, The Bucket, La Playette, and storied evenings of communal imbibery faraway from the academic rigors of the university that awaited anyone who had in his possession an ID that was passable in the dim light of the bouncer's rostrum.

One of my classmates ran an enterprising phony ID business in his dorm room, for five bucks magically transforming birth dates, turning eighteen-year-olds into twenty-one-year-olds. The first time I went along with some older friends to The Bucket with my newly minted ID, I wore my baseball letter jacket to assist the illusion that I was certainly older than my nineteen years.

The bouncer took a quick look at me, checked my ID, stared at me for what seemed like a full minute, then snorted and laughed, "Right—you're good, kid."

I entered to the pulsing beat of Booker T and the MG's "Green Onions," a song I'll forever associate with that memorable night where the beer was cold, the girls were hot, and (as Tom Petty was later to sing) the future was wide open.

There were red flags. I was pretty sure my first college roomie was an alcoholic. His friends told me he'd been a heavy drinker all through prep school, which meant he'd been drinking steadily at least since he was fourteen. I rarely saw him sober, and watched him start bar fights and get his butt kicked by tougher and more sober guys. There were men who partied hard and missed a lot of classes with hangovers. I had never had one so I didn't know how debilitating they could be.

There were friends who would join the monks at unnamed locations for all-night bull sessions where theology, philosophy, and Cold Spring beer were constants. There was a good friend, a roommate, whose drinking would suddenly trigger an irresistible urge to find a car—any car—and drive hundreds of miles to see an old girl friend.

But I was an athlete, and no small part of the indoctrination to membership in Club Jock was the stern prohibition against alcohol and tobacco products. Not that I could have found the money to support either habit, even if my tastes were inclined to Camels or Calvert. It was financially untenable.

Other than the occasional post-game celebration where the local brew flowed like water and tasted about the same, my collegiate drinking career was mercifully uneventful and downright boring. Unlike some of my friends, most mornings I could remember quite clearly where I'd been the night before and how I'd returned to my dorm.

Now at my first teaching job, with a steady paycheck that ensured I could buy a round for my new friends whenever I felt like it, I jumped into the social scene with both feet. Small-town Minnesota social life in the sixties centered on the public high school. At least three nights a week, sporting events were followed by social gatherings at the local bars. Football games, wrestling matches, basketball games—all were heavily attended not only by the community but by the teachers whose charges were playing that night. I happily joined the throngs at the bars afterward, bonding with my fellow teachers and the locals who seemed to enjoy our company. There were a half dozen first- and second-year teachers on that faculty, a result of the school board's funding philosophy that demanded as many entry-level salaries as the superintendent would allow.

Being young and single in a town with a population numbering 1,200 people meant that virtually anyone of dating age was related to at least one of your students. This was certainly the case with the rural beauties that populated the beer joints of this little burg on the prairie.

It wasn't far into the school year when I found myself late on a Wednesday night at a table full of revelers at the Legion Club. The slightly built math teacher had fallen off her barstool twice at that point, and some friends had thoughtfully propped her up against the wall in a booth and tossed a jacket over her head.

Suddenly a hand-held school bell clanged out over the din and the bartender loudly announced, "All right people, listen up! It's 1:00 a.m., closing time, and you either have to go home or I'll pull the shades, lock the doors, and you can stay here as long as you want! What do you want to do?"

"PULL THE SHADES, PULL THE SHADES!"

The chant was joyous and instantaneous, cribbage boards and cards appeared, and the party continued. At 5:00 a.m., the head of the English Department invited the remaining debauchees to his house for some coffee, eggs, and deer sausage, and the Legion Club-turned-speakeasy emptied out for a free breakfast.

My co-renter at Elsie's house, Russell the football coach, joined me for some desperately needed victuals, and at 6:30 a.m. we went back to our place to change clothes and get to our classrooms by 7:30, arriving as the buses were emptying out and the kids were pouring in.

We realized immediately that over half the faculty was missing. The superintendent was pacing up and down the halls, asking us if we knew where Jerry, Bob, John, Barb, Jim, and Jackie were.

"Nope, no idea." I was acutely aware that my mouth was full of cotton, my temples throbbed, and my legs were made of granite. Classes were rung to order, and I assigned some very important reading to my first-hour English lit class and galloped to the water fountain. Ted beat me to it. He took a quick drink and said, "You're a first- year guy, here's a tip: don't make too many trips to the fountain, it's a dead giveaway that you're hung over."

By that time we knew that twelve teachers had called in sick, and there weren't enough substitutes to handle the crisis. Later that day, a note went out to all, reminding us that further incidents like this during the school year would be dealt with firmly, with dismissals and firings an option if the superintendent concluded that another Bacchanalian revel like the one that just occurred at the Legion Club was the reason some students were being left without supervision while others were sitting in classrooms fronted by painfully hung-over adults thoroughly unprepared to teach anything to anybody.

That was a long day at work. I got through it, thinking at the time that I was able to "handle" it better than most, not foreseeing that this particular addiction was going to be a common experience in my chosen profession for some years to come.

4

CATCH 21

I had graduated from St. John's University in Minnesota in 1964 with a BA in English and a four-year course of study in ROTC, the Army Reserve Officer Training Corps. Many of us at St. John's took advantage of the chance to graduate with a second lieutenant's commission in the Army. It required two years of active duty after graduation to fulfill our commitment to the government and help repay the twenty-five-dollar-a-month support we got through our junior and senior years.

We could all see the military buildup and hear the warlike sounds emanating from Washington concerning the "communist threat" in Southeast Asia. It just made sense that rather than be drafted and serve as a grunt private, why not wear officer's bars, eat better food, and get a decent paycheck every month for two years. It was an option we private university chaps had that wasn't available to everybody (a much smarter route to making the system work for you). And that twenty-five dollars a month in our junior and senior years was big money.

We were privileged boys to begin with, camped out for four years at an exclusive, wooded, and laked private Catholic college in an idyllic setting in central Minnesota. We were in the company of 1,200 other middle class fellows who looked just like us, our biggest worries were finding a ride into town on weekends and coming up with a good-enough fake ID to get into the local watering holes.

Classes in military science that would lead to a smoother route to military service with better food and more privileges seemed like just another little entitlement that the system, in its wisdom, provided for us. We would be leaders of men, with better accommodations and fancier uniforms than the privates and corporals in our charge.

A big part of the four-year course in creating thousands of twenty-one-year-old Army officers was summer boot camp. The eight-week basic training course was designed to give us a taste of what the real grunts in our real Army command would experience: physical intimidation, personal humiliation, and the removal of all previously acquired moral and ethical standards relating to the value of human life other than your own or those of your fellow soldiers.

Fort Riley, Kansas, was the summer hellhole chosen for the college boys' initiation into military manhood. Marching, shooting, bayonet practice, accompanied by continuous verbal harassment by regular Army drill sergeants until they had us screaming "Kill!

Kill!" every time we clumsily stabbed a straw dummy on the obstacle course; early morning assemblies, twenty pull-ups in the chow line before you were allowed to eat, 95 degree summer nights when we'd drag our mattresses out of the stifling barracks onto the lawn to try to sleep.

I'd heard from a former teammate who'd gone through the Ft. Riley Follies the previous summer that if I tried out for the camp baseball team and made it, I'd be excused from many of the tougher drills. Baseball teams need to practice, too, although the "Kill! Kill!" chant was discouraged during batting practice.

Upon arrival in mid-June, I immediately found out when tryouts were being held, and I showed up. I'd been a decent pitcher back home, but a shoulder injury made it impossible to make the team that way. So I shagged fly balls like a maniac and hit the ball all over the park, somehow convincing the manager that I was a natural outfielder. I made the team.

Two days later I was on the rifle range, sweating from the pain of the M-1 recoil on my damaged shoulder, when a truck pulled up and somebody yelled "Sieve! Get in, baseball practice!"

I hopped on, joining a dozen other lucky soldiers, and spent the rest of the day swinging a bat and chasing down fly balls. Perfect. This was going to be a summer unlike any other.

I was not a particularly effective Leader of Men. One hot July day, I was told I would be the company commander of a troop of soldiers who were going to take an occupied hill from the "enemy."

They were in defensive positions awaiting our attack. The trucks drove us out to the disputed piece of Kansas real estate, we jumped off, the men assembled around me, I read the map and divided them up into squads and routes to take the hill from the enemy soldiers who were dug in above us.

At my signal, my troops advanced, firing blanks, crawling through brush, hiding behind trees, covering each other, and moving relentlessly up the hill into a surprisingly passive enemy resistance. "This is easy," I said.

Soon all three of my squads had crested the hill without losing a man, and I quickly set up a perimeter defense to protect our hard-won hill. The drill sergeant in charge of the exercise approached me and said, "Captain Sieve? Look over there."

I looked a hundred yards to the west and saw twenty or thirty enemy soldiers looking back at me. I had carefully studied the map and triumphantly taken the wrong hill. I failed the exercise. On the bright side, I didn't lose a single soldier.

So I hid my military shortcomings behind my baseball uniform all summer, only occasionally coming up lame from the damaged cartilage in my right knee. But always able to walk it off and play another day.

The shoulder was another problem altogether. On the rifle range again one afternoon, I was grimacing in pain, trying my best to finish my required rounds at distant targets so I could put that goddamn weapon down and tend to my hurting shoulder joint.

I was interrupted by the officer in charge of the exercise: "What's wrong, Sieve?

"Nothing—just some shoulder pain from the recoil."

"What's wrong with your shoulder?"

"Nothing sir, just a little sports injury."

"Come with me, we'll take care of it."

I followed him fifty yards to a tent on the opposite side of the range, and when my eyes adjusted to the dim light I found I was sitting in the medic's tent.

A full colonel stepped out from behind a table and said, "What's the problem, Cadet?"

"Just a little joint injury, sir—probably from playing baseball. It'll be all right."

"Damn right it will. Take off your shirt."

He went back to the table, and I stripped off my sweat-stained shirt, looking up in time to see the colonel was back with what looked to me like a medieval torture device. A long—impossibly long and thick, at least six inches—needle protruding from a fully loaded syringe containing a milky liquid.

"Where does it hurt?" he barked.

It was clear to me that he needed that information pronto. And it suddenly dawned on me that he didn't believe me and thought I was trying to get out of the exercise by faking an injury.

"In the shoulder, sir."

That was a mistake. Without warning or even decent aim, he

plunged the enormous needle deep into my right shoulder and emptied the syringe. The pain was excruciating, I immediately saw little black dots creeping into my periphery vision, the precursors to passing out.

He pulled the needle out and said, "Now, do something you couldn't do before. Give me some pushups."

I dropped to the ground and did three quick pushups, convinced if I didn't perform he might reload and stab me again.

"Good. Get back to the range."

I somehow made it through the rest of the day; the shoulder felt like the needle was still in there. I laid back on my cot that night and dreamed of lawyers.

And many years later, lying on my sofa, watching an episode of *Mash*, I heard Hawkeye Pierce summarize the effect of my Ft. Riley Army training experience: "I will not carry a gun, Frank. When I got thrown into this war, I had a clear understanding with the Pentagon: no guns. I'll carry your books, I'll carry a torch, I'll carry a tune, I'll carry on, carry over, carry forward, Cary Grant, cash and carry, carry me back to Old Virginia, I'll even 'hari-kari' if you show me how, but I will not carry a gun!"

The summer ended uneventfully, the camp baseball club lost the championship game 9–1. My heroic throw from center field to home plate cut down what would have been their tenth run.

At graduation, we marched around a field with flags and properly shined shoes and polished brass buttons, saluted anybody who looked important, received our temporary "commissions," and drove back to our homes, the hardest part of our military training behind us.

5

DODGING A BULLET

Four years out of college, I was teaching English at my third Minnesota high school. This latest community willing to take a chance on entrusting their kids to me was located right off Highway 94 in the heart of Lake Wobegon, familiar farm country and only a half hour down the interstate from the university that taught me all I knew.

It was 1968 and my right knee became the most significant joint in my body. That's not a punch line. Banged up and rendered unreliable by years of playing baseball and never quite learning how to slide properly, it simply gave out at inconvenient moments and I'd sink to the ground. A few minutes rest and shaking it out, it was weak but slowly, over a couple of days, returned to normal.

I was shepherding a confident group of seniors through a college-prep English class. I had also been corresponding with the US Army, who in its wisdom was insisting that before it would give

47

me my second lieutenant's bars I had earned by successfully completing my four years of ROTC courses, I needed to submit to surgery on my occasionally faulty right knee. I consulted with my doctor, saw a knee specialist, and both told me there was no need for surgery.

Yes, it was true, I might have some loose cartilage floating around in there, what former college jock didn't? But my knee function was serviceable and would likely remain that way for a long time. The reaction by the Army to my refusal to schedule the surgery was simple, direct, and ominous: "Unless you have the operation, we will classify you 1A. You will be subject to the draft."

This news was mildly upsetting. The original purpose of my completing the ROTC course work had nothing to do with any deep feelings of patriotic duty. My reasons were, true to my parent's training, extremely practical. The choice, I thought, gave me a better chance of staying alive were I to somehow end up waist deep in the middle of a rice paddy in Southeast Asia.

My dad served in the Philippines and saw the worst of war. He said many times that although he wouldn't take a million dollars for the experience, he wouldn't pay a dime to do it again. I was more than a bit uncomfortable with the militaristic mind-set in the country, especially as its consequences for men of my age were playing out every day on the evening news and in the papers.

Vietnam was on everyone's lips, in every café conversation. Campuses nationwide were in open rebellion against the draft. The ultimate goals of the war were unclear, but the coffins and broken bodies arriving stateside every day were real, and the numbers were mounting daily. I put it out of my mind that fall as I started the school year, hoping they would just forget about me.

One day in the middle of October, an official-looking envelope arrived in my mailbox, the notice I should have seen coming. I had been drafted. The Army would have its 170 pounds of flesh, including one damaged knee. My draft physical was scheduled two weeks later in St. Cloud, Minnesota.

I would have leave to my teaching job, the safe and comfy confines of my little farming community, and be shipped off to basic training. And if I somehow made it through that, I'd be sent to the front lines not as an officer, but as a lowly private, my hard-won military training and advanced tactical skills wasted, my original brilliant plan upended. I was to be cannon fodder, my personal self subject to the whims of people I didn't know and didn't trust, all in the service of some vague and unconvincing arguments about domino theories and saving the world from communism.

I had lost a teaching job the previous spring because some concerned citizen in another little farm community was convinced I was a communist. I had been outspoken about my students' right to express themselves openly, a concept I mistakenly assumed was at the bedrock of American civic life and one of its most cherished values. The school board declared itself unanimously unwilling to further subject the community to the subversive dangers presented by a graduate of a progressive Catholic university.

Like most young men my age, I was not mentally prepared to travel halfway around the world to seek out actual communists and kill them. I had never met one, seen one, or talked to one. I had no clue whatsoever what a communist looked like or what he might want with my country or its resources, or how communism was in any possible way a threat to our way of life.

I had a childhood memory of my father telling my mom that Joe Sisterman, a bachelor who lived alone near the church, sometimes read *The Daily Worker*. But Dad's comment was more in the context of "Joe is an interesting guy, fun to talk to. He reads a lot."

I had a professor at St. John's who was rumored to be a socialist, which to the minds of some of my classmates lined up nicely with being a communist. But I had found the prof to be erudite, a man of peace, a fascinating speaker, not in the least bit threatening, and more concerned with teaching and supporting his wife and ten children than overthrowing the system.

I tossed the draft notice in a desk drawer and went about my teaching duties, slipping quickly into a state of denial, determined to deal with this development in my life only when it became necessary, and no sooner.

I drove to my parent's home in Alexandria, Minnesota, that weekend and had a long conversation with my dad, a decorated World War Two veteran. He was upset, more than I thought he would be, to hear I was drafted. He knew I was his anti-war son and especially anti-this-war. He didn't believe this war was a just war. He thought it was a terrible waste of people and resources, and fought for the wrong reasons. He didn't want any of his sons to be victims of the bad decisions being made by politicians in Washington who he didn't like or trust. He surprised me when he told me he'd support me in whatever decision I made about the draft notice. He told me if I wanted to move to Canada, he'd do what he could to help me make that happen.

I was touched and grateful, but knew I wouldn't be doing that. I was anti-war, yes, but as far as I knew I wasn't a conscientious objector. I hadn't thought it through to the point where I could put myself in that category.

Dad and I had more than one heated discussion of this country's role in the world since the days he risked his life to stop the Japanese in the Philippines and came home with medals and malaria. We didn't agree on all of it, but he understood that this war was different. The goals were muddy, the price in blood and treasure was too high, the bad guys harder to identify, the motives of the politicians too transparent. But in general, he still believed America was essentially trying to do the right thing.

One afternoon in his living room, I made the mistake of using the word "imperialist" to describe our country's actions in many parts of the world and, from his easy chair across the room, he fired that month's *Reader's Digest* at me and hit me in the chest.

Mom caught up with me in the kitchen and quietly spoke her mind. "You cannot talk that way to your father. We know you think differently, but he has been to war. He risked his life for this country, and he's seen things he hopes you will never see."

I apologized to my dad and went back to work the following Monday, resigned to report for the draft physical and deal with the outcome. One step at a time from this point on, let the chips fall where they may. I had high school friends who were serving. Their lives were on the line. This was the country we lived in, and if it was my duty and I could get through the training, so be it. I would be the best soldier I could be. And as long as they didn't ask me to take a hill, I might even be a good one.

Right about this time, I learned what was to become a critical life lesson: much like the Lord, random chance also works in mysterious ways. Tuesday morning I was standing at the blackboard in my classroom, covered in chalk dust as I sailed through one of my favorite lectures on the Romantic poets. I was moving back and forth between the notes on my desk, highlighting important points on the blackboard. As I pivoted back to my desk to ask a Very Important Question about Lord Byron's inspiration for *She Walks In Beauty*, my old reliable right knee gave way. I hit the floor with a crash, tipping over the wastebasket as I tried to grab it to cushion the fall.

My students rushed forward, assuming I'd had a heart attack. "Are you all right, Mr. Sieve? What happened?"

I struggled to my feet, leaning on the desk and waiting for some strength to flow back into the joint. It always took just a few minutes and, even though it might be weak for a while, I could still put weight on it and function. "No, I'm okay, just an old baseball injury, I'll be fine."

I took a seat, assigned some work to the kids, and rubbed my knee to get some circulation going. This was the first time in many months I had experienced any problem with it. A simple pivot from the blackboard to the desk and *bam!* Down like a sack of rocks. I limped off to lunch where a friend of mine suggested I should have it checked out. I called a doctor and got an appointment after school the next day.

By the time I woke the following morning, the knee was tender but good enough for walking. I put in a full day at school and showed up promptly for my appointment.

The doc took a long look, poking, flexing, stretching the leg, and asking for any signs of discomfort. His verdict: there was some ligament damage, but nothing too serious. If it was up to him, he'd put my leg in a cast for ten days to immobilize it, and that should do the trick.

That's when the light went on in the back room of my cerebrum. My draft physical was scheduled for Friday. It was now Wednesday afternoon.

I asked carefully, "If I decided to let you put my leg in a cast, when would you do it?"

"Oh I'd have my nurse do it right now. We'll put you in a room on the second floor while it dries, and we'll have you out of here tonight."

Well, Mom didn't raise any dummies. (That wasn't Mom's opinion, but her five dummies were all sharp enough to live on the edge of town.)

I said, "Okay, let's do it."

An hour later, from the promised hospital bed, I asked the nurse for the phone. I dialed the draft office in St. Cloud and told the voice on the other end that I was in the hospital, and my doctor would be sending them a notice of treatment of the knee in question for these past four years. My physical should probably be rescheduled. I was acutely aware that a draft dodger is not somebody who simply tries to stay inside during windy conditions. Sometimes, fate dictates the definition.

Two weeks later, another official-looking envelope arrived, I opened it and was informed I'd been re-classified 1Y, to be drafted "only in case of a national emergency." (Specifically, if they found an actual communist trying to sneak into the country.)

I had dodged a bullet. As it turned out, quite a few bullets and more than a few mortars, grenades, and land mines. I was not unaware of the ironies.

If the Army had simply ignored my usually reliable knee and accepted my statement that it was good enough to be awarded my commission, if they hadn't insisted on surgery, I might have been an infantry 2nd Lieutenant in Vietnam, a position that accounted for some horrendous mortality rates over the course of that war. I began to fully grasp Hamlet's truth: "There are more things in heaven and earth, Horatio, than are dreamt of in your philosophy."

More than once in my life since that October, I have thanked whatever better angels were watching over me for the break I was given. Many young men of my generation weren't that lucky. The ones who made it back still carry a heavy load.

The school year droned on, I had only one more incident on the basketball court with my knee. The buildup in Southeast Asia continued, draft cards were going up in smoke across the country, and America confronted itself and its leaders on a wide range of issues on its role in the world and its relationship to its own history and ideals.

6

THE DOUBLE DUTCH

By 1969, with a new lease on life and any of my previous anxieties about dying early in the jungles of Vietnam safely out of mind, I had decided to either (1) live wild, fast, and free; travel the world; fall in love; and write the Great American Novel; or (2) sign another teaching contract.

So being first and foremost my mother's pragmatic oldest son, and fully aware of her version of "wild, fast, and free," September found me back teaching English and directing plays in Stearns County, Minnesota.

One of my duties involved coordinating visiting musical acts and variety shows booked by the administration for the student body in the interest of brightening and broadening their cultural horizons. These were usually serious professional performances. My job as the drama teacher was to meet with the artists, see that the audio and

56

lighting setup satisfied their needs, and generally make them feel welcome at our little rural school.

One particular show that arrived on a snowy day in December, a brother/sister folk act from the Netherlands, was about to make this a memorable year. Roberto and Maria were an energetic Dutch acoustic duo who sang songs in six languages. They'd been brought to the States by Peter, Paul and Mary to open for that famous trio on one of their many US tours. When the Amsterdamers were no longer needed on tour by PP&M, they decided to stay awhile longer in the US and book some high school and college gigs.

Peter Yarrow got them an agent, and this was how they found themselves at a Stearns County High School for a one-hour afternoon show in the middle of a Minnesota winter. Roberto had broken his ankle in a fall on an icy sidewalk, but gamely carried on with his music.

Maria was a vivacious redhead with a mysterious smile and an exotic accent. Despite the language barrier, we communicated . . . well. (I try not to overuse the ellipsis, but there is no other way to arch my eyebrow in print.) When the Dynamic Dutch Duo found out I played guitar and sang American folk songs, they questioned me relentlessly about the artists I followed and whose music I covered. Their catalog of American folk music was limited, and I think they saw me as a resource. They promised to stay in touch but when they drove away that afternoon, I assumed I had seen the last of them. But not so!

The exotic, mysterious Maria and her brother, Roberto Van Lint, the opening act for Peter, Paul and Mary in Alexandria, Minnesota, 1968.

A week later my phone rang. It was Roberto, telling me that he and Maria were doing a college show a half hour away and wondering if I would meet them for dinner that night. I gladly accepted. The thought of seeing the alluring Maria once again was more than a small consideration.

At dinner that evening in St. Cloud, Roberto waited till Maria excused herself to find a restroom before telling me that his sister found me "interesting" and would like to see me more often.

"Really?" (Did this exotic international artist know that I was an underpaid teacher with no connections and an uninspired wardrobe? That I spoke exclusively English with only a passing acquaintance with French?)

Roberto said, "She likes you. She's been away from home for months. She hasn't had a date since we've been in the States. She wants to make music with you."

The various connotations of making music with Maria unfolded instantly in my reptilian brain, and my pulse quickened. At the end of the evening, I promised Roberto I would find him a date the following weekend, and we would double-date for dinner and a chance for Maria and me to discover more about our musical interests.

I called a friend of mine who was enrolled at St. Cloud State University, told her I was looking for a date for a personable and talented international visitor on crutches, and could she find a friend of hers who might possibly be blonde and bilingual, two conditions that Roberto had tasked me with. She called back the next day, and yes! Roberto was in luck.

So at dinner the following Saturday night, after some excellent wine and good vibes all around (Roberto and his date, Chris, were speaking French and having a wonderful time), Roberto sat back in his chair and offered me the opportunity of a lifetime. Would I like to perform with him and his enchanting sister at the wedding reception of Peter Yarrow and his bride-to-be at the Willmar Country Club the following Saturday?

"Peter Yarrow? Of the Peter, Paul and Mary Yarrows?"

"Yes, my friend, that one," he said.

Peter had asked his friends, Roberto and Maria, to entertain the guests during the reception after the ceremony where he was to take Mary McCarthy, niece of the illustrious Senator Eugene McCarthy of Minnesota, as his lawfully wedded wife. And they were now asking me if I'd like to join them with my guitar.

"Are you kidding?" I croaked. "Absolutely not."

Roberto and Maria completely understood my reticence. I was not only not a professional musician; they were asking me to join them—professionals—to play in front of three of the most famous professionals in the country. What a nightmare that would be, having my strikingly average voice and guitar technique exposed for the world to hear and to be politely tolerated by the legendary Peter, Paul and Mary. I would be more than excited to accompany my Dutch friends to the wedding and reception, but under no circumstances would I bring a guitar or a banjo or even a triangle. *No no no no.* It might be just peachy for Bob Dylan, but in my experience nothing good happens when you ask a tambourine man to play a song for you.

I was a big fan of Senator McCarthy. I had begun a personal political awakening a year earlier as the Vietnam War brought people into the streets, and the good senator from Minnesota faced off against Lyndon Johnson for the nomination in the 1968 presidential election campaign.

I was driving from St. Cloud to Fulda, Minnesota, the night of March 31, 1968, in my blue Delta 88 Oldsmobile when Johnson's announcement crackled through the AM radio: "I shall not seek nor will I accept the nomination of my party for president."

I stopped by the side of the road near Paynesville and hooted into the night sky: he did it! McCarthy did it! The man was a hero to me, and I was sure he'd be at his niece's wedding.

Thus it happened one week later. I sat two rows from the back of St. Mary's Church in Willmar, Minnesota, and heard Paul Stookey sing, for the first time in public, a song he wrote for his good friend, Peter Yarrow, "The Wedding Song (There is Love)."

It was remarkable, unforgettable. It was the first of millions of weddings where that song would be sung. And even more memorable, an hour later when the bride asked all of us at the reception at the country club to take a seat on the floor because Peter, Paul and Mary wanted to perform an *a cappella* version of their new song, "Leaving on a Jet Plane" as a gift to the bride.

I sat with Roberto and Maria, six feet from three giants in American folk music, and heard the best version of that song anyone had heard before, or since I am sure. As Paul Simon sang much later, *"they blew that room away."*

Sixty days later, "Leaving on a Jet Plane" was the number-one song in the land.

Noel Paul Stookey, Peter Yarrow, and Mary McCarthy in Willmar, Minnesota, October 18, 1969. Photo courtesy of *West Central Tribune.*

John Lennon famously said, "In the end, everything will be all right. And if it isn't all right, it isn't the end." My doomed romance with the multi-talented, multi-lingual, full-lipped Maria ended some weeks later when she and her brother returned to Amsterdam to pursue their careers. We parted wistfully, promising to meet again but knowing it was unlikely. The geographic realities of our chosen lives and professions would no doubt prove insurmountable. And it was all right.

There was another ending a couple of years later (again, all right) when my folk-singing career concluded after an audition at a club in downtown Minneapolis. Duff's was a popular Minneapolis watering hole whose main floor most nights was occupied by the professional athletic community, the Vikings and Twins and their hangers-on.

Upper Duff's was a small, intimate black-curtained room with a tiny stage, a stool, and seating for no more than fifty. Just the kind of place I had once imagined I would use as a launch pad for national notoriety by singing John Prine covers.

The club was looking for a fill-in folk singer to work a Thursday night gig. The manager heard me do a couple of songs and said, "Fine, be here by eight thirty, you'll start at nine."

I had spent a few evenings at Upper Duff's, listening to some impressive performers, one or two with recording contracts and recognizable names. I went home excited, ready to start work on the four sets of covers I knew I'd need later that week.

But that night, I had a dream—a bad one. Something about starting a song at Upper Duff's with a full room, and by the time I played the final chord of "Sounds of Silence," the place was exactly that: silent and soundless. Everyone had left. *What the hell was I thinking?* I wasn't a folk singer. I was a teacher, possibly an actor, but certainly not a folk singer. I'd never written a song. This wasn't Stearns County, this was *Hennepin* County, the big time. People here knew the difference. They'd expect to hear *real music* as they nursed their overpriced drinks. They'd snicker. I'd be humiliated. *There would be no free blackberry brandy.*

My insecurities were in full flower. Panic was setting in. I called Duff's the next day and told them I couldn't make it. That was the last time I took my guitar out in public. And the world was better for it; trust me on this.

7

BUS TRIPS AND ACID TRIPS

Sometime around the Christmas holidays that year I got a letter from my childhood best friend, Dave Lenderts. He was living in Washington DC, attending medical school, and he invited me to visit him and catch up with our lives.

I had never been to the nation's capital, hadn't seen Dave since the mid-fifties when I moved from our little town to the farm in central Minnesota. I had nothing planned for the Easter holiday school break, so I booked a ticket and eagerly awaited spring vacation and a reunion with my old childhood buddy.

I arrived one warm spring night when the cherry blossoms were in bloom along the Potomac. I got a cab to Dave's apartment in Northwest DC and ascended the stairs to the fourth floor, where I found a note on his door, telling me he was out bird-watching along Rock Creek and to make myself at home. It was still early in the evening; and although I had no idea where I was in the city relative to the monuments and famous capital locations I wanted to see, I set out to explore the neighborhood and see where I might end up.

The first thing I noticed strolling down 14th Street was an unsettling number of burned-out buildings. On several street corners there were small crowds of people being addressed by men with bullhorns.

I needed to find the Lincoln Memorial, the White House, the landmarks I associated with this city, so I approached a young woman at a bus stop and asked her where I could catch the bus downtown. She gave me a strange look, didn't say a word, then moved quickly across the street. She left me standing there to figure it out on my own. *Hmm.* Odd.

I decided to hang right there for a bus and ask the bus driver how to get where I wanted to go. My patience was rewarded shortly after when a city bus pulled up. I jumped on and asked the driver. He told me he would end up where I was heading, and to just sit down and he'd tell me where to get off.

I took a seat, noting immediately I was the only white person among a dozen passengers. At every stop, more people got on, and no one sat near me. We proceeded along a route I hoped would get me to a recognizable landmark.

Ten minutes into the trip, I saw what I'm sure was clear to everybody else: I was still the only white face on that bus. I clearly remember thinking that this vague sense of unease gnawing at me must be an everyday experience among African Americans in

Minnesota. I lived and taught in the center of the state, 100 miles from the Twin Cities. There were certainly no black Minnesotans where I lived. I was twenty-six years old, and the term "white privilege" had yet to enter the lexicon. I only knew my life up to then had been free of any need to adjust my thinking, habits, speech, or daily routines to any other group of people—or to what they might be thinking or how they might react to my skin color.

By the time I hopped off the bus, it was full and I was still the only Caucasian in sight. I wandered around the familiar landmarks and monuments for an hour or so, then retraced my route back to Dave's apartment.

When I arrived, he welcomed me with a beer and asked me where I'd been.

"Just took a stroll through the neighborhood, ended up down at the Washington Monument. Took the bus."

Dave sat down and stared. "You did what? You went for a walk?" He shook his head. "You are a lucky man, my friend."

"What? Why?"

"Did you notice the neighborhood? Most of it burned out the night Martin Luther King was shot. In this part of town after dark, you are not welcome. What were you wearing?"

"This." I was still dressed in the sandals, shorts, and the baseball warmup pullover I arrived in.

"They must have thought you were an undercover cop. You really shouldn't have done that. I'm sorry I didn't tell you, it isn't safe here for guys like us at night."

I told him about my odd encounter with the young woman at the bus stop, and he said there was no way anybody would have engaged me in conversation. I stood out in that neighborhood like rat droppings in clear soup.

And so began my very first field trip to the political, racial, and cultural streets of the American 1960s. I had traveled little to that point, thought little about anything other than my small corner of the world in Minnesota.

Dave's apartment was set up to smoke dope and drop acid: comfortable furniture, an elaborate Indian carpet hanging on the wall, drug paraphernalia on a low table in the living room where a small group could sit cross-legged, load a bowl, and drift off in a haze of smoke to the sounds of Janis Joplin, with Big Brother and the Holding Company blasting from Dave's massive speakers.

In the five days I hung with my old friend, I was informally introduced to the city of Washington DC via David's old green Volkswagen Bug. The starter didn't work, so we had to park it facing downhill in order to let the rolling start engage the tranny when we popped the clutch.

But he showed me the city, introduced me to the joys and small terrors of an acid trip, and we talked into the night. We covered everything from Hindu philosophy to the evils of war and the benefits of a vegetarian diet.

He taught me how to cook up a tasty pot of dhal, which, after a couple of joints, was the most insanely delicious food I'd ever eaten.

I went back to my little central-Minnesota town with an altered perspective of the world. I was becoming dimly aware that, despite John Denver's claim, life may be more than just *"a funny funny riddle."*

8

PAYING DUES

I had only done a couple of plays in college, small and forgettable roles in long forgotten productions. Even with that thin resume, I was deemed experienced enough to direct the theater program, such as it was, at my first high school teaching job. I quickly became a self-taught director, learning on the job. I read books on stagecraft, how to build flats, perspective, design, lighting. Six years and three schools later, I had directed over a dozen plays, acted in several community productions, and felt that, at the age of twenty-seven, I had the chops to move confidently to the next level: professional theater.

An actor friend of mine encouraged me to show up at a TCG (Theater Communications Group) audition in Minneapolis where I would find dozens of producers and directors looking for actors for their upcoming seasons. I put together a comedy monologue and did my three-minute audition, expecting to be ignored.

To my surprise, I was offered a full summer season of plays at Mankato State University, including a lead and a good character role. It was an unpaid summer, but I'd be getting graduate credits in theater toward my master's degree. I pounced on it.

June of 1969 found me crouched onstage at the Highland Summer Theatre in Mankato in the role of the dim, unkempt Lov Bensey in *Tobacco Road.* It was a good piece of casting, requiring mostly monosyllabic grunts and nods. I knew I could do that.

The memorization was a breeze, and it gave me a chance to get my feet wet in a semi-professional setting without a lot of responsibility. This production, however, was doomed by an unfortunate choice for the lead role of Jeeter Lester, the father of a hardscrabble family of sharecroppers in a desolate part of Georgia in the 1930s.

The actor playing Jeeter looked and sounded perfect: sunburned bald head, a scraggly fringe of hair graying at the edges, tobacco-stained teeth, hair growing out of his nose and ears, and a gravelly, nicotine-damaged voice. No one knew where he came from or what his background was, but he looked like he was born for this role. Even his name was perfect: Ayres McGrew.

This was summer stock. We had four shows to mount in an eight-week season. Rehearsals were long and intense, and prep time was at a premium. It took only a few days for the cast to realize that Mr. McGrew was never going to accomplish the most basic task an actor must complete: learn his lines.

The first week of rehearsals passed and all of us were off book except Jeeter. Dr. Ted Paul, the director, a Minnesota theater legend, was concerned but patient. The rest of us were sharing the stage with this guy, and we were panicking. Three days out from opening night, we got together with Jeeter and told him we were going to take turns running lines with him in our individual scenes, and we'd do it until he was secure and comfortable in every scene. He had the lion's share of the lines and they needed to be drummed into his head with as much repetition as we could manage in the few short days we had left.

The next day, we opened the Ayres McGrew Crisis Center as each of us in the cast took turns taking him aside and running our lines. When my turn came, we got three lines into our first scene when he stopped and asked me where I was from. I told him. Then he asked about my college background. I told him. Then he needed a bathroom break. Then a drink of water.

We restarted the scene. He stopped and asked me about my family. We started again. Then he needed a cigarette break.

I realized with dawning horror that he knew he was in over his head and didn't know how to deal with it. I tried to get him to focus on the scene, to simply run the lines. He suggested we take another break and get a cup of coffee. I gave up and went back to the stage and sent in the next actor.

When the play opened a few nights later, the theater was sold out. The music and lights came up, the curtain rose, and all of us stood by and watched Ayres McGrew drive our production straight down Tobacco Road right into the ditch. As each scene unfolded, Jeeter would spit out a line or two, go completely blank and walk over to one of us and whisper "What's my line?" It was horrific.

We all did what we could, we knew his lines well enough, but that two hours and twenty minutes was an actor's nightmare. It all finally came to a head in the second act when Jeeter staggered upstage to Captain Tim Harmon, who had come to tell the Lester family that the house and property were owned by the bank, and whispered his now expected pitiful request: "Line?"

The actor playing Harmon crossed his arms in disgust, pointed at me standing at the other side of the stage and said loudly and firmly "Talk to him!"

All of us, along with the play, collapsed.

The reviews were not kind. I still remember the first line of the article in the local paper, written by a guy who later became the head drama critic for the Minneapolis *StarTribune*. It simply said, "Shame on you, Ayres McGrew." That had a nice lilt to it, I thought. Well said.

The second play in that summer series was *A Delicate Balance*, a Pulitzer Prize-winning play by Edward Albee. The role of Harry, a visiting friend of the lead couple, Agnes and Tobias, was being played by a thoroughly annoying actor with a ridiculously pretentious name—let's call him Forrest, that sounds about right— who embodied everything non-actors dislike about theater folk.

He was egotistical, narcissistic, selfish, demanding, lazy, and the least-popular person in the company. He was also the victim of one of the most well-executed show pranks I have ever had the privilege to witness.

It was opening night, and Harry was standing by the upstage door that served as the front entrance to Tobias and Agnes's living room, waiting to make his first entrance with his wife, Edna. One of my friends, Bruce, who played the fed-up Captain Harmon in *Tobacco Road*, had heard Forrest/Harry expound on his theories of acting. Bruce watched as Forrest belittled other younger actors, and was not at all fond of this preening twit. Bruce was working as a stagehand in this production. He was standing near Forrest as the time approached for the doorbell to ring and Harry and Edna to enter.

Bruce leaned over to Forrest and asked quietly, "Are you nervous?"

"Of course not," he snapped back.

Bruce leaned in and said, "Well, you should be; you're not very good, you know."

The doorbell rang, Harry and Edna entered, and Forrest blew his first three lines.

The wind had been taken out of Forrest's sails, and for the remainder of the summer, he walked more softly and talked more carefully around everyone. A small bit of humility had been served up, and he seemed to digest it well.

The Pajama Game came and went without incident, and finally it was time for me to step into the lead role of the prosecutor in *A Shot in the Dark.* This play was a far cry from the Peter Sellers movie farce in that the lead in the theatrical version was more a romantic leading man than a comic character.

I had a thousand lines, and only a week to learn them. I was onstage for all but two pages.

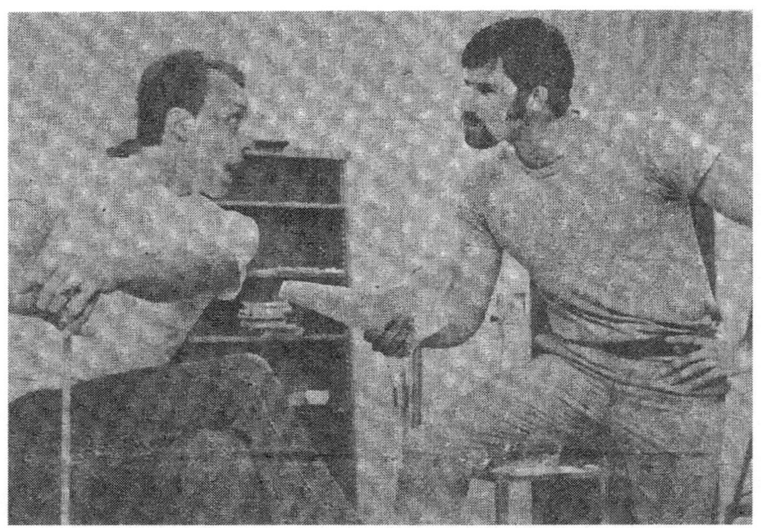

Interrogating a witness, *A Shot in the Dark,* 1969.

The ingénue, the French maid, was being played by a first-year drama student from the Twin Cities. The young blonde actor looked the part, but she was a bit short on experience.

I had been working night and day to memorize this role, I'd never had this much responsibility onstage. It was difficult, but a real opportunity to show what I hoped I could do. What made it especially tricky was the series of interrogations the prosecutor conducted at the witness chair directly stage center. All the questions for each witness were similar, with minor variations depending on who was being interrogated. By tech rehearsal the day before opening, I was finally solid on the lines. I knew this thing. I was not going to be a younger, hairier Ayres McGrew.

Opening night found a packed house, and we launched Act One. The comedy was playing well; we were firing on all cylinders. The French maid was brought into the prosecutor's office, seated in the witness chair, and I began the questioning. Stalking my prey while my assistant took notes at his desk stage left, I questioned the maid rapidly and efficiently.

Three minutes into the scene I asked a key question about her relationship to the murder victim. There was a long pause. She looked at me as if she hadn't heard the question. I repeated it.

Suddenly I realized I was a Mack truck bearing down on a baby fawn. She had no idea what her line was and neither did I. But I needed her response to move on to my next question. It was my cue, and I didn't know the scene well enough to know my line without that all-important cue. I paced around the witness chair.

The silence was dramatic. Even though it was still the first act, the audience must have thought this was a key moment in the play. I repeated the question. Still nothing but silence and building terror from the maid. I looked across the stage to the prosecutor's assistant, an excellent character actor named Rick, a graduate student in theater who had been a rock all summer, a sturdy and dependable guy with a lot of stage experience.

He saw we were in trouble, got up, and motioned me to a spot directly behind the witness chair with the frozen blonde in it. *Thank God*, I thought, *he knows the line!*

I lurched over to meet him, he leaned into me and whispered into my ear: "*Bzzzbzzzfurzzzmmmttt.*"

He didn't know crap, he was just creating a little stage business to stall for time. Three hundred fifty puzzled patrons were getting restless. I turned back to my desk, shuffled some papers importantly, strode back to the witness and asked the next question I could think of. She responded! Thank God. We moved deftly on with the scene. There was something about it that wasn't quite right, but we got through Act One with no further difficulties.

During the brief intermission, however, we were told the awful news: we had cut thirteen pages out of the first act, including the scenes of two characters who hadn't even been introduced yet!

The play ended surprisingly early. The audience liked it but, because of the critical exposition they weren't allowed to see, there were some puzzled reactions at the cast party that were unfairly blamed on the playwright.

Dr. Ted called a meeting and was explosively angry, directing his fury straight at me, the guy who was supposed to ask the right question. He was right. I took the blame, I was older, supposedly more experienced. I should have been able to get us back to the right place in the script. But I didn't. And I was mortified. No one except me, the stage manager, and the lighting director in the booth knew that it was the maid who did it. She was young, so I took a bullet for her. It was a far, far better thing I did than I have ever done. I said. Dramatically.

9

MR. WEBB AND THE
BIRTHDAY GIRL

That summer gave me an insight into what it might mean to someday be a real working actor. Long hours, intense rehearsals, short time frames in which to devour many pages of dialogue and commit them to memory. Summer stock is one of the great little secrets of the profession, a concentrated immersion into the total theater experience—from building sets to designing and building costumes, learning the tricks of makeup, latex, and facial hair, and performing one script while learning and rehearsing the next one. I loved it.

I returned to my teaching job determined to keep not only a toe in that theatrical water, but both feet whenever possible. My work in my little Central Minnesota town suddenly seemed more constricting and no longer the direction I now envisioned my life should be heading.

The solution? Keep directing plays, keep acting when possible, and do more summer stock as soon as the opportunity presented itself. And the following summer, it did.

After another successful audition, I found myself at an established, respected summer stock theater in Alexandria, Minnesota: Theatre L'Homme Dieu, named for the lake on whose pine-shaded shores it was built. The lilting French name had long ago become Midwesternized and was pronounced *La-homma-doo* by the local residents. Visiting actors and directors from New York were looked on with suspicion if they used a French pronunciation.

Theatre L'Homme Dieu was founded in 1961, and in the summer of 1970, it already had a rich history of presenting strong professional theatre to the Alexandria Lakes area.

The Texas and Oklahoma owners of summer homes on the surrounding lakes had become accustomed to attending well-produced and well-acted productions of Broadway shows after a day spent fishing and water-skiing. The Theatre L'Homme Dieu campus was a former resort that was converted into a theater campus with housing for thirty-eight, a lodge with an industrial kitchen, and a 272-seat proscenium theatre. The campus sat on 22 acres of wooded land, with access to beautiful Lake L'Homme Dieu.

The original idea was smart: partner the theater with St. Cloud State University, a reputable college 60 miles away, and let the excellent University theater department, headed by the legendary Dr. R. Keith Michael, run the place and use students to do the technical work, make the costumes, build the sets, and fill in the smaller roles. Finally, hire a core of pros from the Twin Cities and New York to perform the leads.

I was far from what I considered a professional actor at twenty-seven. I had only done one summer of comparable work. But Dr. Michael saw something in my audition that convinced him I would be a good addition to his core acting ensemble. He offered me several small roles and one plum: playing Henry VIII in Robert Bolt's *A Man For All Seasons*. I thought I was too young to play the rotund monarch, but Dr. Michael's idea was to play him as a young Henry, before all the feasting, drinking, and debauchery turned him into the Falstaffian caricature we see in his typical artistic representations.

My parents had bought a restaurant in Alexandria three years before, and it had been successful enough for them to buy a lake property the following spring only a mile from the theater. I agreed to come to Alexandria for the summer, as long as the University allowed me to stay off campus in my family's lake cabin.

This was an unusual request—actors for the most part were required to stay in dorms and lodges on site. It was easier to run a theater that was producing eight plays in eight weeks if you had the worker bees all assembled and under control in one hive, eating, sleeping, rehearsing, and performing together. For some reason, they said, "Sure. You can stay off campus."

That was a mistake they would regret.

The first day of rehearsal, I was introduced to an intense and well-spoken blond actor my age, recruited from the Actors Theater of Ohio University and brought in to play the lead, Thomas More, in *A Man For All Seasons,* along with several other good roles throughout the summer.

Ray and I became instant friends, sharing especially a love of basketball. He was a West Virginia native, where basketball is the official state sport. We'd find time before and after rehearsals to go one-on-one in the summer heat till we dropped from exhaustion. I represented Minnesota well. I was four inches taller; he was quicker. Our games were always close.

Our rehearsals for *A Man for All Seasons* began immediately. It was the opening play of the summer, and I found myself trying to keep pace with an actor whose training and understanding of the stage was light years beyond mine. We had only one scene in the play, but it was a long and intricate little dance between the historical giant of a monarch who demanded absolute loyalty from his subject and the man whose conscience wouldn't allow him to give it.

King Henry's overarching and unpredictable temper dominated the play's action and its outcome, and the scene was critical. We worked hard at it, squeezing every drop of drama out of each line. At one point, Henry takes out an ornate dagger from a sheath at his belt, gestures with it, and makes his point by slamming the knife into the wooden tabletop where Thomas More is sitting.

On opening night—with my palms sweating from the anxiety of our first public performance, the heavy fur, leather, and brocade costume and the 90-degree heat in the non-air conditioned theater—the dagger slipped out of my hand and landed at More's feet. *Hmmm.* That was unfortunate. Now what?

A short pause, and to my surprise and relief, the quick-thinking Thomas More bent over, picked it up, and in the perfect actor's solution to the little onstage accident, went to one knee before his king and presented the dagger to him. The perspiring Henry slid it back into the sheath, ad libbed, "Thank you, Thomas," and the scene went on nicely.

As Henry VIII with unreliable dagger, with Thomas More
in *A Man for All Seasons,* 1970.

That opening production kicked off the summer perfectly. It sold tickets, and the audience on the final Sunday night performance would see one more little incident with the infamous Royal Knife that would stick in their minds for days to come.

By now Ray and I were locked in and running smoothly through the scene each night, Henry was throwing his temper tantrum, Thomas was maddeningly reasonable. We were doing Mr. Bolt's script proud. At the moment when Henry returns his dagger to the sheath, I gave it a little extra dramatic shove for emphasis—and it went straight through the thin leather sheath directly into my left hand, opening a large gash at the base of my thumb.

Probably because the performance adrenaline was pumping strong, I barely noticed, but I was bleeding. Alarmingly. So when Henry slammed his left hand on the table in front of More to make his final point and threatening his death, bright red royal blood flew everywhere: in More's face, his costume, into the front row, all beautifully lit and as real as it ever gets in the theater.

Henry made his exit up the stairs, blowing his exit line: "Affairs of court call me to state" [no, you idiot, affairs of STATE call me to COURT], which caused Thomas More to turn his face briefly upstage and snicker. I was met offstage by an assistant stage manager with an armload of bandages and towels. More's eyes were large, but he wiped off the king's blood, and the play proceeded.

That summer was memorable for more than the accidental blood-letting. Gatherings at the lake cabin a mile away hosted by Henry VIII became a weekly event, usually after the Wednesday night opening of the next production.

Word got back to Dr. Michael of alcohol, loud music, late hours, and the occasional naked actor running down the lawn, along the dock, and into the lake, a veritable *Animal House* with St. Cloud State University's name attached to it. The host of these extra-theatrical evenings—the brilliant twenty-seven-year-old actor so committed to his craft that he shed blood to perform King Henry—was fast becoming singularly unpopular with the administration. (It wasn't my fault that Thursday morning's rehearsals were slower, more hung over, more thirsty than other rehearsal days. But the University did hold me responsible.)

As far as I know, I was the last actor in the long-and-storied history of theater *luh-homma-do* to stay off campus.

One final, notable highlight of that summer occurred on the closing night of Thornton Wilder's *Our Town*. I had a small role, playing the town constable, and Ray was playing Mr. Webb, Emily's father. Today a smart producer would double-cast some of the roles to save some money, but there was no shortage of University students to play townspeople, farmers, and professors. We had a full cast of twenty-five actors populating Grover's Corners that week, all of them swarming around backstage and dodging each other to make entrances and exits.

The actor playing Emily was a lovely, angelic twenty-something from New York who had made it her apparent summer's goal to sleep with every willing male cast member on campus. She was going through men like kids go through peanut M&Ms.

We were only halfway through the production schedule and she had already exhausted most of her possible targets. She was currently batting her large eyelashes at one of the older members of the stage crew.

Ray and I had stayed safely out of range, he was involved with another woman in the cast, and I had a girl friend who was spending the summer in Michigan.

There's a scene somewhere in the middle of *Our Town* where an excited Emily Webb and her family are preparing for her birthday celebration, and Mr. Webb is heard offstage before we see him, calling out, "Where's my girl? Where's my birthday girl?"

I was standing stage left that night, watching the scene unfold, and Ray was ten feet behind me, preparing for his entrance. Seconds before his cue line, I heard him hiss, "Hey! Sieve!"

I looked over my shoulder to see him standing near the wall in the dim light. He had placed himself strategically at a spot backstage where he was only visible to me and no other members—*er*, citizens–of the Grover's Corners community. With a firm left-handed grip on his limp Little Ray, he said his line, "Where's my girl? Where's my birthday girl?"

I fell to the floor in a seizure of merriment as he tucked away his equipment, zipped up, straightened his tie, and walked out into the light to join the birthday celebration for Emily. The instant legend of Mr. Webb and The Birthday Girl was a story with only one privileged eyewitness to its veracity.

Summer stock. It's a long eight weeks. You gotta keep it interesting.

❧

Theatre Le' Homme Dieu is extremely proud to have Mark Sieve return to its stage after an absence of six years. Longstanding patrons of the theatre will remember Mr. Sieve for his outstanding performance as Henry VIII in the 1970 production of A MAN FOR ALL SEASONS as well as his appearances in OUR TOWN, THE PRIME OF MISS JEAN BRODIE and CACTUS FLOWER.

Currently teaching English, Physical Education and Creative Dramatics at Folwell Junior High in Minneapolis, Mr. Sieve is a 1964 graduate of St. John's University in Collegeville with a B.A. in English. He has taken extensive graduate work at St. Cloud State University and Mankato State University in speech and theatre.

Mr. Sieve considers Alexandria to be his "second home" and regular habitat. In 1967 his parents, Ben and Helen, moved from Long Prairie to Alexandria and presently operate The Traveler's Inn with his two brothers, Jon and Kurt, in the downtown area.

To Theatre L'Homme Dieu, Mr. Sieve brings an extensive list of theatrical credits. In Minneapolis he has appeared as Banquo in MACBETH, Alan in THE BOYS IN THE BAND, Naumovitch in ALEXANDER'S DEATH and Colin in IN CELEBRATION, all at Theatre in the Round. He appeared as DeSota in THE ROYAL HUNT OF THE SUN at St. Paul's Chimera Theatre and performed as Hopgood in the Chimera West musical production of HELIZAPOPPIN.

For the St. Paul Opera Workshop he was Mr. Bumble in OLIVER and also helped establish the Melrose Minnesota Community Playhouse.

At the Children's Theatre Company in the Minneapolis Institute of Arts complex he played the role of Orsino in TWELFTH NIGHT, and has performed in THE HAPPINESS CAGE, THE PORNOGRAPHIC SAMPLER and the musical DAMES AT SEA at The Cricket Theatre. While at the Cricket Theatre he promoted their production of HARVEY by appearing as the title character in numerous downtown Minneapolis and St. Paul locations.

Mr. Sieve is an accomplished fencer, having studied with Guthrie Theatre alumnus Erik Fredrickson, and performs regularly with fellow Theatre L'Homme Dieu actor Joe Kudla. Their Shakespeare Comedy Fencing Duo is already scheduled for the forthcoming Renaissance Fair in Chanhassen, Minnesota. With Twin City actor Phil Morton, he created the comedy due MORTON AND SIEVE, presenting singing, dancing, vaudeville sketches and satirical revues for private parties and various civic functions.

Educational television showed his performance as The Doctor in TWO CASES FOR RAPE and he also created the role of Chuck for the Stuart Rosen teleplay of MATRIX. Commercially he is known to television viewers in the state, having appeared in the advertising of The First Bank Systems and Montgomery Wards.

An avid outdoor sports enthusiast, Mr. Sieve is a member of the Hegg's Heroes Softball Team, made up almost exclusively of Twin City performers, and enjoys snow skiing and motorcycle touring.

This summer Mr. Sieve also appeared as Dirk Winston in MARY MARY, Charlie in NEVER TOO LATE, Jonathan in ARSENIC AND OLD LACE and as Hogan in UNDER THE YUM YUM TREE.

I returned twice in the next six years to my favorite theater by the lake. St. Cloud State decided to take advantage of the marketing opportunity that presented itself in advertising a returning local boy whose family lived and worked in the community.

They offered me lead roles in plays like *The Front Page, Arsenic and Old Lace, Mary Mary, Never Too Late,* and a half-dozen more, all giving me a chance to stretch my stage legs and do roles no one else would have cast me in anywhere else. The local paper gave me far too much attention; even smaller roles drew interviews, newsprint, and bio paragraphs in the program that seemed to go on forever.

Other actors rightfully wondered what was so damn special about Sieve that was worth all that ink. I agreed. It is atypical, to say the least, to see the details of an actor's family's lives, where they lived and where and when they moved to another town, in a program resume.

We were still producing seven or eight plays every summer. Amid the chaos of daily rehearsals, midweek openings, Sunday closings, installing new sets on Monday, and final tech rehearsals Tuesday night before the Wednesday opening, there were still unscripted adventures popping up with predictable regularity that had to be dealt with.

One hot Sunday afternoon, I left my parent's downtown restaurant and headed to my car. It was closing night of *Under the Yum Yum Tree,* and I wanted to get to the lake and take a nap before the show. I stepped off the curb and instantly felt a hard and extremely painful muscle pull up the left side of my back. It took my breath. I leaned on the car and steadied myself.

Any movement at all was excruciating. I slowly crawled into the driver's seat and made my way to my brother's house a few blocks away to get some help. I found his sofa and laid down. No relief.

We decided it was bad enough to call a doctor. My brother suggested a chiropractor he knew and called him. The doc was having a backyard party but told us he'd meet me at his office as soon as I could get there. I half walked and crawled back to my car, got to his office, struggled inside, collapsed on his table, moaning and trying desperately to find a position that stopped the stabbing pain.

The doc was drunk. Or at least halfway there. He gave me a tortuous and cursory back "adjustment" and sent me on my way. I was pretty sure he made it worse.

By now it was an hour from curtain, so I drove to the theater, staggered to the dressing room, sponged on some basic makeup, got into my wardrobe and made it backstage, where I stood, bent over, leaning on a chair, then lying on the floor, still trying to find a position to stop the wrenching pain.

Dick the director arrived and presented the possibility that we'd have to cancel the show. It was sold out, my family was there, but how the hell could I do this show when every time I opened my mouth to speak or move I'd gasp as if someone had just gut-punched me.

Dick said, "This isn't going to work, you're really messed up, I'll announce we're cancelling."

I didn't want to be responsible for the theater losing a full night's receipts just because I suddenly forgot how to walk down a street without hurting myself, so I said desperately, "Why don't we start the show (*gurk*), I'm not on for the first five minutes (*groan*), maybe I can stand like this (*ouch*) and improvise a reason for it in the first scene (*oof*)." I stood, leaning grotesquely to my right side like a drunken sailor.

He said, "Okay, give it try. But if you're still standing like that ten minutes in, we'll have to stop the show and give them their money back."

The first scene of *Under The Yum Yum Tree* has a young couple arguing in the living room of their attic apartment. Shortly after the play starts, their landlord Hogan—me—is seen listening at the keyhole.

I decided to stay bent over at the door in full view of the audience. Just before my cue to knock, I would stand up and pretend to wrench my back, then play it that way as long as I could and see if the audience bought it. It was weak, but all I could come up with. I stepped into the light on cue, bent over to listen, stood up to knock, grimaced broadly, and made my entrance, still half-hunched over on my right side like Quasimodo.

Luckily, I had accidentally found a position that didn't hurt too badly, or at least didn't cause further spasms. Again it was likely the adrenaline that takes over for many actors when they walk onstage. I made it through two-and-half hours of a performance that night that no one in the cast, including me, ever thought would happen.

"Working" on the grounds of Theatre L'Homme Dieu, '70s.
Yes, those are bell bottoms. Why do you ask?

I felt like a warrior. I went out front to greet my family, and my brother said, "Interesting choice to play that character like he had a broken back."

"Yes, thanks," I said, adding, "His 'back' story is all about a spinal fusion he got after the war."

This enchanting little summer theatrical escape in the lake country of North Central Minnesota was like perpetual recess for an actor, a place to play and compete and invent and create in a setting that encouraged all those things at once. And it laid the groundwork for a longer, deeper career on professional stages I once thought were beyond my reach.

10

ACTING UP

Back in Minneapolis, opportunities were popping up with regularity. I grew a beard to add a few years to my cherubic cheeks and quickly began picking up roles I probably had no right to play, given my age and experience.

I entered my "serious artist" phase with a full head of steam, and even started smoking an occasional cigarette to complete the image I was trying desperately to project. Other than college-related summer stock, academic training credentials were noticeably missing from my resume. Many actors I worked with had BAs in Theater from the University of Minnesota and other auspicious theater programs. I suspected I needed some Shakespeare to broaden my appeal to directors of the classics, so I auditioned for a production of "the Scottish play" at Theatre in the Round.

Yes, the Scottish play. You can't say the word "Macbeth" to anyone in the cast when you're actually rehearsing or performing a production of the Scottish play; it's considered horrible luck.

Serious actor phase, early '70s.

Theater stories abound of actors dying of heart attacks onstage during the show or being crushed by falling scenery backstage, or walking out of the theater and getting hit by a bus—all because someone said the word "Macbeth" in the theater.

Even whispering the name of one of Shakespeare's bloodiest plays inside a theater is a serious taboo. I did it one night (a thoughtless accident) in the dressing room during a performance of *Spinning Into Butter* in St. Paul. Three actors instantly shouted at me to shut up, one of them spun around in a circle, muttered a counter-curse and mimed tossing salt over his shoulder. Another actually ran outside, danced around three times, and spit on the sidewalk. And these people are erudite and experienced professionals! (Another technique to counter the possibly disastrous effect of saying *you-know-what* is to recite out loud any line from *Two Gentleman from Verona*, considered by most to be one of Shakespeare's lucky plays. Seriously.)

There are any number of reasons why speaking the play's title in a theater is considered bad luck: the spooky invocations of the witches, for instance. If you believe that Shakespeare adapted these spells from actual books of black magic, it's easy to see why this may have opened the play up to forces of darkness that can come back at any time and haunt productions of . . . the Scottish play.

Another theory holds that the actor playing Macbeth in the original production died in an accident, and Shakespeare himself had to go on in his place. Some believe that all subsequent productions are now haunted by this actor and his melancholy fate. Some people also believe that if you accidentally sit on a camera, you can get Polaroid's. I'm not in either camp. The theater is awash in superstitions and traditions like this. I suppose it adds to the mystery.

If you spend any time at all around actors, you'll find there are any number of taboos you can innocently violate, bringing down the wrath of the more knowledgeable on your bewildered head. There are—in the minds of the dedicated thespians—sprites and goblins in every theater who love to mess with actors and will take whatever sincere expression that's verbalized into the exact opposite of what is wished. If you inadvertently say "Good luck!" to a fellow actor just before the opening night curtain, these nasty little fairies may somehow find a way to make the opposite of good luck happen, like maybe break your leg. Thus "Break a leg!" as an opening-night salutation should nicely thwart these theatrical spirits. Wish for something bad, they will have no choice but to provide something good. Makes sense to me. I'm a former Catholic, so I'm used to relegating everything I don't truly understand to the category of "mystery." Another theatrical superstition involves lighting, as in "turn on the ghost light." Theater people believe you should never leave a stage entirely dark. In practical terms, there are always set pieces, props, trap doors, and orchestra pits that could lead to serious accidents in the dark. Now this is a long theatrical superstition I can sink my teeth into.

During a preview of *Pure Confidence* at Mixed Blood in 2009, I delivered my melodramatic line that ended the first act, and in the ensuing blackout I stepped to my left to exit. Since it was still a preview and the stage manager hadn't had time to place a small blue ghost light offstage as a target, we found ourselves in total darkness. Naturally I misjudged my direction and found myself in mid-air heading for the first two rows. It was a spectacular fall, loud, messy, and painful.

Fortunately the seats were unoccupied. As I tried to get up and disengage from the tangle of chairs, a friend of mine who was in the audience that night and sitting just two rows from where I landed said quietly and firmly in the darkness, "To your left. Go left."

I did, and I stumbled to the dressing room to lick my wounds, both physical and psychological. Once again I got lucky, nothing broken, but that night I became an eager proponent of the ghost light.

There is a second, more historical and practical explanation for the need for a ghost light. When theaters were first lit, before electricity in the early nineteenth century, the lights were powered by gas. This gas could build pressure in the lines, so burning the flame of a ghost light even during non-performance hours burned off excess gas and eliminated the pressure that might result in an explosion. Gaslighting is gone—other than what we get from our politicians—but the tradition remains.

More superstitious theater people also believe that the ghost lights help to keep spirits at bay, so there is that.

Superstition and theater taboos aside, I auditioned for the Scottish play and was cast as Banquo. The large cast was uneven—some obvious pros in the larger roles, less experienced younger actors in smaller parts. The set design was unfortunate—a long, circular ramp that started a few inches off the floor and circled around several times to the height of four feet—finished off with a strange, alien aluminum pole that extended at an angle to the ceiling. The result being that no matter who you were speaking to in the play, you were both on opposite sides of a pole.

Macbeth himself was played by a large-voiced actor who looked and sounded the part, but whose personality was just a few therapy sessions short of psychotic. We never knew when he was being Macbeth or just that weird bearded dude who yelled a lot.

Lady Macbeth was being played by an oral interpretation professor at the University of Minnesota, a short bespectacled woman with long black hair who delivered every speech like she was announcing a fire in the theater.

At the first rehearsal read through, our director stopped us at the first scene with the Three Witches and said, to the consternation of all, "We're going to cut the 'double double toil and trouble' speech; it's trite and nobody needs to hear it."

We all looked toward the witches (one of whom I'd already developed an interest in and was hoping would be the one to help me with my Scottish accent). They were staring at each other with all three mouths slightly ajar. One of them finally spoke up. "*Um,* excuse me, but those lines are why I auditioned for this play. Wouldn't that be kinda like cutting Hamlet's 'To be or not to be' speech because most people were familiar with it?"

The director held his ground until two of the witches stood up, put down their scripts, and began putting on their coats. "If you cut those lines," one said firmly, "I'm outta here. The only reason I want my daughter to see me in this play is to hear me say those words."

After some hurried apologies and promises to reconsider, they sat back down and the read-through went on.

There were a few other moments during the rehearsal process that to more-experienced actors would have been warning signs that sent them scurrying out into the night, leaving their scripts fluttering behind. One occurred a week later during a work-through of Banquo's scene with his son Fleance, just before they're set upon by Macbeth's hired killers, and Banquo is dispatched. Shakespeare's themes in the Scottish play are well known: darkness, blood, treachery—the night is murky, overcast. Fog and gloom seep out of every scene.

Banquo says to Fleance, "There's husbandry in heaven, their candles are all out." Meaning, of course, that no stars are visible, it's pitch black, the "candles" of the stars are hidden. That's the husbandry part—thrift in the heavens.

On cue, the line came out of my mouth and the director stopped me. "Mark, picture what they're seeing. They're looking up at this beautiful sky, the stars fill the heavens, it's a spectacular night. Keep that in mind as you say that line."

I stopped. The cast looked at me. Suddenly in that moment, we all knew we were leaderless and rudderless, adrift in an impending Shakespearean tragedy that would only be a tragic mistake for the audience. I decided not to argue, even though he had just spectacularly misinterpreted the whole scene. He thought Shakespeare meant that the stars were *out*. Not "out." *Oh my effing God.*

A few nights later, the same director informed us that Banquo would be entering the banquet scene in ghostly form with a bloody sheet over his head. Like a Shakespearean Casper the Friendly Ghost. You could hear the room gasp.

This time I was saved from having to decide whether or not to start an argument because the unpredictably mercurial Macbeth suddenly roared to life and announced that if Banquo's ghost was appearing in a sheet like we were doing some kind of goddam high school version of this play that he, Macbeth, was walking. Out the effing door.

It took awhile, but order was restored and rehearsals went on. The bedsheet idea was scrapped and the decision was made to keep Banquo as a figment of Macbeth's fevered mind, as it is often played. A close call. The critics had enough ammunition already; we didn't need to make them laugh out loud.

We opened to tepid reviews, deservedly so. The critics

recognized the unfortunate confluence of bad design, bad direction, and bad acting. Lady Macbeth's line, "Take my milk for gall you murdering ministers," was so over the top and funny that several of us backstage would start a low chorus of *"Everybody needs milk."*

The circular ramp and pole kept getting in the way of the final sword battle between Macbeth and Macduff, so much so they finally shortened it up and Macbeth was dispatched long before the fight choreographer had originally planned. But it was *theater,* it was honest-to-God *Shakespeare.* The costumes were lovely and appropriate. The Three Witches were excellent. The actor playing Macduff went on to a distinguished stage career in Canada.

Sometimes you have to crawl before you walk. E'en tho 'twas tatties o'wer the side, thankfully I still had a sultry witch to spend some evenings with, working on my Scottish accent, laddie, or the whole dighted, bowfie mess would ha' been irredeemable.

⁂

This was a rare stinker of a play at a good theater that actually became my Minneapolis College of Theatrical Knowledge. Even then, Theatre in the Round was an established Twin Cities training ground for actors who had yet to gain their Actors' Equity Association card, but were doing plays that were giving them valuable experience working with good scripts and, often, good directors.

With the luminous Camille D'Ambrose in
The Prime of Miss Jean Brodie, TRP, '70s.

The work was unpaid, but it was important work. It was the first Minneapolis theater to cast me after I moved there in 1971. By the time I got my card as a union actor some years later, I had stockpiled a number of strong roles in plays such as *Boys in the Band, In Celebration, The Real Inspector Hound, Who's Happy Now?, The Prime of Miss Jean Brodie, Alexander's Death, Steambath*, and the unfortunate Scottish play.

The Boys in the Band, TRP, '70s

The experience at TRP (Theatre in the Round Players, Inc.) was priceless. Some of the actors I had a chance to share the stage with moved on to long careers in Chicago and on both coasts. TRP is still turning out excellent work to this day. I recently saw a production of Arthur Miller's *A View from the Bridge* that was the best of this play I'd ever seen on any level.

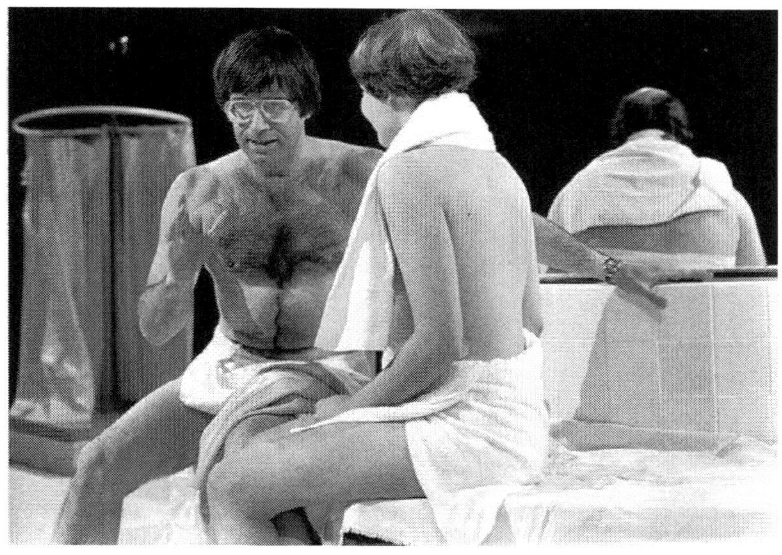

Steambath. I see dead people. In transition with Christy Meyer, TRP, '70s.

After the near career-ending experience with the Scottish play, my next Shakespearean effort came soon after, playing Orsino in *Twelfth Night*, a much more competent and entertaining effort directed by the late Charles Nolte and produced at the Children's Theatre Company. Nolte's vision for this production set the play in the Middle East. The opening scene featured me as a nearly naked

Arabian prince onstage in a bathtub being attended to by draped and veiled women while belly dancers and musicians swirled around me.

As the music swelled, Orsino stands up in the tub and proclaims, "If music be the food of love, play on!"

Surprisingly, no one laughed. I spent the weeks before opening doing situps and pushups like a madman, in the sure knowledge that at the opening line of the play all eyes would be on the scantily clad Prince of the Desert. I was determined the Prince would look like he could actually have earned his harem.

I played The Herald in a Variety Hall production of *Marat/Sade* in St. Paul. One of the Twin Cities reviewers wrote a few lines that—if I took him at his word and believed he knew what he was talking about—could help shore up any doubts I had then about carving out a career in this stage thing. Tom Gifford of the St. Paul *Pioneer Press* wrote, "Sieve's Herald is witty, dispassionate, arrogant, posturing, performing grandly at every opportunity and holding the whole business together, making sure none of the points are blurred or missed. There are difficult theses in the play, and the Herald must delineate them. Sieve is tremendously at home in the role."

Why thank you. I didn't realize at the time I was doing all that, but maybe, just maybe. . .

A series of roles at the new Cricket Theatre in Northeast Minneapolis, in plays with titles like *The Pornographic Sampler, Dames At Sea, and The Happiness Cage* added some needed heft to my resume, giving me the confidence to step it up a level. I auditioned for and was cast in a production of a little-known Irish play about a Welsh coal miner and his three sons, *In Celebration.*

The lead was played by an Irishman, Cecil Allen, a meteoric actor from the University of Minnesota. I had never encountered someone like Cecil, an actor who could go off script at any moment and whatever came out of his mouth, even though it often wasn't the playwright's words, was somehow better than what had been written for him to say. It was startling, often brilliant—but certainly unsettling for those of us who were listening for the exact cue line.

The reviewers knew they were watching someone unusually gifted. The *StarTribune* reviewer wrote, "Theatre in the Round opened its 24th season over the weekend with an engrossing production of David Storey's *In Celebration*, thanks to a whirlwind performance by Irishman Cecil Allen in the play's catalytic role."

Cecil and I became fast friends and decided shortly after the play closed to create our own theater company. We had no idea how to go about it, but as most actors would, we picked a playwright, selected a couple of Pinter one acts, and found a church on the south side of Minneapolis that housed the Guild of Performing Arts where we could rehearse and stage them. We called ourselves Theater Co-Op. We hired a director and a terrific actor, Barb Granning, and went to work.

As you can tell by the press release, we didn't have any money. Phrases like "no-frills theater" and "concentrating on acting and directing quality, not spectacle and finance" appeared prominently. At a ticket price of $2.50, there was an excellent chance that we'd still have no money when it all ended.

FOR IMMEDIATE RELEASE: CONTACT: Laurie Johnson
October 27, 1976   333-8269

THE LOVER and THE DUMB WAITER by Harold Pinter
presented by the Theatre Co-op
Friday and Saturday, November 19 and 20   8:00 P.M.
Guild of Performing Arts Theater
504 Cedar Avenue, Minneapolis

Theatre's not new to the Twin Cities. But the Theatre Co-op is!
The Theatre Co-op will present The Lover and The Dumb Waiter --
two Harold Pinter one-acts on Friday and Saturday, November 19
and 20 at 8:00 P.M. in the Guild Theater.

But don't look for grand theatrical spectacle at any Theatre Co-op
production. Mark Weinberg, director, said the new company will
concentrate on acting and directing quality -- not spectacle and finance.
The Theatre Co-op allows semi-professional and professional actors
and technicians a chance to learn and perform in a "people-centered"
theatre environment, said Weinberg.

Acting and directing is at the heart of drama, not frills. And that's
what's at the grassroots of the Theatre Co-op.

Well-known local community theatre actors, Cecil Allen, Barbara
Granville and Mark Sieve will be featured in the Pinter one-acts which
mark the debut of the Theatre Co-op.

Additional performances will be held at the Walker Church (31st and
16th Streets) on November 11, 12, and 13. All performance times are
8:00 P.M.

Tickets: $2.50 adult/ $2.00 student and senior citizens.
         MAT Vouchers accepted for full admission.
Reservations: Call 333-8269.

504 CEDAR AVENUE   MINNEAPOLIS, MINNESOTA 55404 * PHONE 333-8269

But we chose a great writer and a solid director, and we rode Cecil's intense stage presence to a happily successful debut. One critic from the *Twin Cities Reader* said, "The Theater Co-Op has a no-nonsense, workshopish feel to it that's pleasantly invigorating for the theater-goer who is sick and tired of being played up or down to. These are serious, talented people working on a craft, and their efforts are worth seeing."

Barb Granning, Cecil, and I have no idea why I'm grinning like an idiot in *The Lover*, Theater Co-Op.

The initial artistic success of our little venture predictably did not translate into financial viability, and the Theater Co-Op opened and closed its doors with that production. Cecil and his wife, Julie, were thinking about moving back to Ireland to raise their children. Without him as the artistic anchor, further productions held no interest for me. It was the mid-seventies, I was making my way through good days and bad in my nascent stage career and in my day job as a teacher in the Minneapolis Public School system. I soon found myself happily immersed as both an actor and director in a newly formed theater company on the West Bank of the University of Minnesota: Mixed Blood.

11

BLOOD ON THE RESUME

Mixed Blood Theatre is located in an ancient firehouse on the West Bank of the campus of the University of Minnesota. The theater was created by my friend, Jack Reuler, who had recently graduated from Macalester College and had shared the stage with us at Theatre in the Round in a production of *Steambath*.

Jack conceived Mixed Blood as a place where minority actors, playwrights, and directors would have an opportunity to act, write, direct, and develop as artists with the same opportunities afforded their white counterparts working in all the other theaters in town.

Jack asked me to direct a new script about Muhammad Ali entitled *The Last Champion*, written by one of his company members, Sharon Walton. My directing to that point had been confined mostly to school and community shows, so I was thrilled at the chance to direct a professional production.

I asked Jack why he wasn't directing the play, as it was his theater. He responded enigmatically, "The cast doesn't want me to direct this one. They want me to find someone else."

Jack was running an oddly egalitarian theater where the voices of the company members carried some weight, and the core company, including the playwright, had decided they would choose who would direct this epic.

Jack told me, "They want to meet you and see if you're the right guy for this. We'll be at Little Caesar's tonight at 7:00. They'll be able to tell if they want to work with you after we've all had some pizza and a couple of beers."

Jack is a dedicated sports fan and was aware of my background in college sports and my familiarity with the athletic world. The actor playing Ali in this show was a former University of Minnesota baseball player, and Jack thought it would be helpful to get a director who could speak Jock to get to the heart of this script. And since we were good friends, he knew he would have plenty of input in the show's direction that I, as a first-time professional director, would welcome.

I arrived at the appointed time for my audition dinner and spent an hour getting to know the Mixed Blood Theatre Company. Jack called me later that night to tell me I had been approved; rehearsals could start forthwith. It was a strong cast, and even stronger production.

Lisa Henricksson wrote this review in the *Twin Cities Reader* with the headline: KNOCKOUT AT MIXED BLOOD:

"*The Last Champion* is unquestionably a fun show knowledgably directed by Mark Sieve. All the things that could work against it end up working for it. It's like having a really good *Sports Illustrated* story jump off the page and come to life in the theater. And that, lest you read me wrong, is high praise."

I got very lucky with *The Last Champion*. Jack had given me a fine cast. Geoff Ewing played Ali (Geoff would later play Ralph Puke for a season at the Maryland Renaissance Festival). Michael Laskin, the best Howard Cosell impressionist in town, played the late great Mr. Cosell. Mike is now head of the Michael Laskin Studio and Coaching in L.A. where he teaches acting to up-and-coming film hopefuls.

Sharon Walton's script was tight and funny. We erected a boxing ring in the middle of the set and choreographed Ali's final fight with Jerry Quarry blow by blow for three rounds. The stage blood was impressive. Ali and Quarry were realistic and ferocious. Cosell was hilarious. It all worked. It was my baptism of fire at Mixed Blood.

I went on to become Jack's "sports director" in the eighties and nineties, directing the baseball play, *Bleacher Bums*; the basketball play, *Ohio Tipoff*; the golf play, *How To Improve Your Golf Game*; and a one-man play about the legendary Minnesota Twins owner Calvin Griffith, called *Calvinisms*.

THE LAST CHAMPION
or
The Third Coming

Mixed Blood Theatre

Ohio Tipoff required us to build a locker room set that somehow created the illusion that the basketball players were larger and taller than they actually were. Jack's idea was to make the lockers and doors smaller and shorter. It was a long-winded script that would have run past three hours. Jack, understanding there was a big risk in asking audiences to sit for that long while minor league basketball players sat around the locker room in their underwear discussing their lives, loves, fears, and futures, told me to cut the script to no more than two hours.

The director explaining how minor league basketball
is like a *Hamlet* production.

I removed every line of dialogue that didn't advance the plot. One hour of fat was discovered and excised. We started rehearsal. I knew immediately that the cast Jack had given me was so good that it would be really a smart move to just get out of their way and let them work.

I had actors that are still, almost thirty-five years later, some of the most prominent names in Twin Cities theater: Steve Yoakam, James Craven, Jim Cada, and guys like GregAlan Williams (now a strong presence in the movie and TV business in L.A.), and Joe Keyes, an L.A. comedian and actor who worked with GregAlan when they did Puke & Snot clones on the East Coast.

The play opened, the players bared their backsides heading to the showers (as is the case in all locker rooms), and audiences seemed to enjoy, *um*, hanging out with them for a couple of hours each night.

The Minnesota Daily review said, "*Ohio Tipoff* is about a fictitious basketball team from Lima, Ohio, called the Ohio Mixers, playing in a real basketball league, the Continental Basketball Association. When Jack Reuler does a sports play, he usually gets Mixed Blood's 'resident jock' Mark Sieve to direct it. Under his direction, the Mixed Blood Company gives this play a breezy, highly competent reading. The performances are uniformly fine."

❧❦

Interspersed with these sporting productions were some memorable plays like *Lemons*, set at a car dealership in the South. This production stands out in my memory as important because its big cast included even more of the Twin Cities most recognizable stage talents, although relatively unknown at the time: Lou Bellamy, founder and artistic director of Penumbra Theatre in St. Paul; Pat O'Brien, longtime movie and television actor and cast member of *Saved By The Bell;* Kevin Kling, renowned storyteller, actor, and playwright; Bob Breuler, now a company member at Steppenwolf in Chicago; and several of us lesser lights.

It's also notable because of what happened one night when Mr. Bellamy, playing a customer who tries to rob the dealership, decided to even the score with another actor, Geoff Ewing, who'd been messing with him onstage, trying to get Lou to break character.

Lou's big scene near the end of the play required him to fire off a warning round from his starter pistol—loaded with a blank, obviously—to show he was serious about getting the money. That night, without telling anyone, he loaded the pistol with six blanks, and when the moment arrived he fired his one shot into the air, then leveled the gun at Geoff, his torturer, and started firing blanks at him and chasing him around the stage, screaming, "Goddamn terrible actor! Always messing around with people! I'm gonna kill you!"

Geoff was genuinely shocked, running off and taking shelter behind the 1963 Moretti parked center stage. Watching this unscripted action from the wings, the rest of us were stunned, but only for a moment as gales of laughter poured out from backstage. Mr. Ewing had been properly terrorized and Mixed Blood's reputation for presenting strong, unpredictable, and sometimes outrageous theater had been fortified.

Lou Bellamy, me, Pat O'Brien, and unidentified customers
in car in *Lemons*, Mixed Blood Theatre.

One other moment in *Lemons* is burned, unfortunately, into my brainstem, a piece of dialogue that at the time we all thought accurately portrayed the characters employed at Beuchel Goodie Motors, the local Edgar and Beamus dealership in some unnamed southern town, but when delivered casually each night brought winces and chuckles in equal measure from audience and cast alike.

O'Brien and Breuler, playing car salesmen working the floor of the dealership, are sitting in their cubicles chatting, killing time. Breuler asks O'Brien what was the most memorable sex he'd ever had.

After a short pause to consider, we heard O'Brien's line, delivered offhandedly as a fond memory: "Fucked a goat once and had a live trout up my ass. [PAUSE, THEN INDIGNANTLY] Not at the same time!"

O'Brien says to this day, it's the most memorable dialogue he was ever blessed to speak in his more than forty-five years of professional life.

∛∞

Being a contract player at Mixed Blood allowed me to peddle my talents to other directors and theaters around town. One unfortunate choice was an audition for a production of Peter Shaffer's *The Royal Hunt of the Sun* at St. Paul's Chimera Theatre.

The play was an historical drama set in 1532 when Spanish con-questador, Francisco Pizarro, leads an expedition into the heart of the Inca Empire, captures the Incan Emperor Atahualpa, and claims Peru for Spain. The movie version had Robert Shaw, Christopher Plummer, and Nigel Davenport.

I was offered the role of De Soto and jumped at the chance to play a conquistador and invade Peru. Chimera Theatre was not an Actors' Equity theater, which suited me just fine since I was not an Equity member at the time. I chose instead to work at whatever theaters offered interesting roles instead of union theaters where the competition for work was much stiffer and the casting possibilities more limited. The flip side, of course, was that non-union theaters had fewer professionals, and even fewer resources. Artistic visions were necessarily constricted by tighter budgets.

If you wanted to portray a Spanish battalion marching down the Andes Mountains to attack a Peruvian village of Incan peasants, the Guthrie Theater could build you a million-dollar set that looked and felt like the Andes. Chimera's budget could build you a wooden platform twelve feet high with steps on each side. Oh well. We had a good cast. I was playing Pizarro's right hand man. Pizarro was being played by a good actor I trusted. Atahualpa was played by a strong actor we all knew and respected. How bad could this be?

Uncommonly bad.

Lou Dezseran as Atahualpa was costumed in full body paint

and what we all thought was a giant diaper. With the exception of their high priest who was outfitted in white feathers with a jeweled crown, the Incas wore burlap. Rehearsals were hectic, disorganized, with many unproven actors playing soldiers and peasants stumbling around the set. A couple of moments from this storied theatrical mash-up will never be forgotten by anyone who was there opening night.

The scene: the Inca village enters by the hundreds, it seemed— to the sound of drums. All the peasants are doing a choreographed fertility dance that slowly fills the stage with burlap-clad and body-painted Incas. The Spanish expedition climbs the mountain stairs to the "peak" (of the platform), stops, and looks down as the dance and the drums end. The feathered and bejeweled high priest of the village walks out through the crowd (now all on their knees and bowed down in postures of reverence), steps onto a small platform where a spotlight hits him full figure. He raises his staff imperiously just as De Soto speaks the following extraordinary line to Pizarro: "Look! That must be their head man!"

There was not a night during the run of this show when that line didn't get a huge laugh from the audience. The end of the first act brought a symbolic massacre of the Incas by the Spanish, choreographed to music that left dozens of Inca bodies sprawled across the stage. Just before the blackout, a huge red cloth (blood, get it?) is unfurled from the top of the platform.

The night it all went south is still talked about in hushed tones.

The massacre plays out, the red cloth is unfurled. There is a full and dramatic blackout to signal the end of the act. The drums stop, and the audience hears an actor scream in the darkness followed by a startling thud as he falls twelve feet from the platform to the stage. In the stunned silence, we hear the clear voice of the stage manager over the house sound system: "WOULD THE OWNER OF THE GREEN BUICK LESABRE LICENSE NUMBER RGL805 PLEASE RETURN TO YOUR VEHICLE. THE LIGHTS ARE ON AND THE MOTOR IS RUNNING."

It happened. I was there.

12

A PIECE OF MEAT

Memorably bad productions like *The Royal Hunt of the Sun* were the exception, thank God, not the rule. The Twin Cities has always had a deep pool of theatrical talent to draw from: directors, producers, actors, and technical geniuses kept the odds of getting involved in a clunker to a minimum.

This pool also supplied a burgeoning commercial video and film industry with a competitive community of actors to make shooting a project in the Upper Midwest appealing to producers and ad agencies who, in the past, had often gone to the default position of casting in Chicago, New York, or Los Angeles.

Commercials and corporate video, always a good source of income for a professional actor, can come with a price. Commercial actors often are hired for their appearance, and nobody gives a damn if they can act. Actors on a commercial shoot where the require-ments are simply "bite and smile" for a food spot, or "turn and grin" for a clothing spot are sometimes treated like pieces of meat. The phrase traces to a legendary actor who, finally fed up with being moved around on a set like a robot, screamed at the director, "I'm not a piece of meat, I'm an ACTOR!" Which, of course, led to the classic joke about the pig hired to shoot a pork commercial, and halfway through the session turns to the director and shouts, "I'm not an actor, I'm A PIECE OF MEAT!"

Sometime around 1974, I got a call to audition for a series of Northern States Power commercials that would feature a lone actor talking about how NSP supplied its customers with electricity. The spots were designed to be simple and direct. The actor stands next to a pile of coal and says, "This coal will light this bulb for five years. This is what we do. NSP. Keeping your lights on since 1953."

I showed up at the appointed time, glanced at a script, found my mark, looked into the camera, and spoke my lines. The director said thank you and I left, not giving it another thought until three days later when my agent called to let me know they wanted to see me again for a callback.

This meant I was in the mix, someone at the agency thought maybe I could sell electricity, and they wanted me to do it again. I went back to the same studio, this time there were only eight actors instead of the original fifty they'd seen, and we each did another take or two and left. This is the time in the process when an actor goes home and starts glancing at the phone, wondering if the next call will be the one that brings home the job, the bacon, the lettuce, the paycheck. I admit that's what I did.

But nothing, no call. Until the next morning. My agent told me that they had narrowed the field to two of us, and they wanted to see me that afternoon for one more callback.

I started to get excited, we'd been told that they were going to shoot a whole series of these spots over the next year and the actor who got the job would have his face everywhere. The NSP Guy: TV, billboards, buses, stadiums, the airport. Everywhere. And that's what it's all about, just ask the Progressive lady. Or Jan the Toyota girl. Or that lucky GEICO gecko.

Lots of media face time equals a full bank account. I went in to take a shower and comb my hair and pluck my nose hairs and brush my teeth and make it impossible for them to not hire me.

When I got to the studio, I was introduced to Nick, a blond actor who'd been working at the Old Log Theatre west of Minneapolis, I'd never seen him work but he seemed like decent sort, a gruff, good-looking dude who probably did most of the young male leads at the Old Log.

He went in first and, after about ten minutes, came out, waved goodbye, and left it to me to do what I could to make them forget about him and cast me as Mr. Electricity. I did my damndest, I became a crackerjack coal salesman before their very eyes.

But the job went to Nick. I got the news the next day. Like all actors, chalked it up to another close call, but a rejection nonetheless. I was okay with it, I knew there would be other opportunities.

Within a couple of weeks I began to see Nick The Blond Scandinavian Stereotype on my TV day after day, night after night, selling me and all Minnesotans on the wonders of NSP power. I started to not like him.

I made some calculations based on the union pay scale for a regional commercial at the time, and this guy was making a shit-ton of money. He might be able to stop working at the Old Log for a while if he kept churning out spots at this rate.

I put it out of my mind and went about my life, auditioning for plays, picking up occasional corporate video jobs and the rare commercial. Somebody told me that Nick had taken his NSP bankroll and moved to Los Angeles. I remember thinking, *Yep, with that cash he'll be able to take his time getting work out there and won't be under any pressure at all.*

In 1976, I tuned into a hot new miniseries called *Rich Man, Poor Man* and saw Nick Nolte, the NSP Guy, in his first big splashy role in La La Land. Local boy made good. He finished that year with Emmy and Golden Globe nominations for Best Actor in a TV series.

From electricity salesman to star. Guess I should have seen him at the Old Log when I had the chance. I was happy for him. That's my story, and I'm sticking to it.

It wasn't till a few years later that I lucked into my own NSP-style series of spots, and I made the best of it. Cable television was making a big push for customers at the time, and their ad agency came up with a character named Traffic Officer Bob, a gruff, no-nonsense law-enforcement type in full uniform who looked into the camera and bluntly warned Minnesotans in the middle of another nasty winter to "Stay warm, stay home, and cable up!"

The audition process was much like the NSP spots. A hundred actors show up the first day and the callback process continued till the ad agency and sponsor had their man. At my first reading for Traffic Officer Bob, I drew upon my memory of a drill sergeant I remembered from my summer of Army ROTC training in Ft. Riley, Kansas.

I channeled Sergeant Hackenmuller perfectly, and I could tell by the quiet conversations among the ad people that I struck a nerve. So after a callback the following week, I wasn't totally surprised that I was now about to have my face plastered on billboards, buses, and benches, and be regular living-room company for Minnesotans for the next year or two.

There was no trip to Los Angeles or a possible series in store, but I was comfortably established in Minneapolis with no intention of risking my mental health chasing the dream. Traffic Officer Bob became my entrée into a lot of other work in the commercial and video industry. I was now a minor "known quantity," and I would ride it till it collapsed.

Here's your
last chance to go
FREE!

Stay Home, Stay Warm
And Cable Up

"Cable up before it piles up."

13

MY THREE MAMETS

After a dozen years of being handed strong roles in strong theaters, working with strong directors, I felt confident enough to tackle any role any director would risk with me. I had done Shakespeare, comedy, musicals, straight dramatic roles, leads, and characters. I had co-created a satirical Shakespearean comedy act that played all over the country. In the mid-eighties, in my forties, I was finally ready for Mamet.

David Mamet, the Pulitzer Prize-winning playwright, whose language was vintage locker room and whose characters were unapologetically avaricious, unflinchingly amoral, and absolutely riveting, was writing plays every actor wanted to do. No American playwright had Mamet's ear for everyday speech.

His characters conversed in verbal snatches and half-formed thoughts. The words were only guides to thought and motivation. His plays took Broadway by storm, selling out performances with stars like Al Pacino in *American Buffalo* and Peter Falk in *Glengarry Glen Ross*.

Mamet wrote plays about truly interesting people. Truly awful people, yes, but that's what made them interesting. The characters he created were universally unscrupulous, self-absorbed, guided by no other God than personal profit. They were uncaring, vicious, without a tinge of compassion and without souls or hope of human dignity. Just the kind of character any actor would love to bring to the stage. Hey, Nana, how do you like me now?

As a young teacher out of college, I had kept an eye out for alternative career paths, knowing that a teacher's salary would, over a lifetime, never allow me to be financially secure. I signed up with a life insurance company to sell their products.

And I discovered after six months that if I needed to depend on my friends and relatives as my main "leads," and after badgering them relentlessly to sit and listen to my sales pitch on Why They Needed This Whole Life Policy Now, I would soon be without friends, and my relatives would never ask me to another family reunion.

I explored selling encyclopedias, but after listening to the bored pitch from the Britannica field manager and hearing what I recognized immediately were deceptive sales techniques designed to convince people who couldn't afford it to fill bookshelves they didn't have with a set of books they'd never open, I declined the offer.

I even became a realtor, literally overnight, the summer I was cut from my teaching job in Minneapolis. This was the second time I was cut and, in a fit of frustration, I decided to explore another career and quit depending on the vagaries of the teacher's union seniority system.

I tracked down an eight-pound book of real estate law, stayed up all night, read it cover to cover, and passed my real estate license test the next morning. *Shazam!* I was a Realtor. For a year I wore three-piece polyester suits, paid for a thousand cheap pens with my name and realty company emblazoned on them, sat at several dozen open houses asking people to remove their shoes, and listed and sold exactly zero homes. I tossed my Open House signs in the trash and focused on my acting career.

Happily, when I finally got the chance to do a Mamet play, my experience with the sales practices involved in *not* selling life insurance, encyclopedias, or real estate became a handy guidebook to the mind of the dealmaker—the world that virtually all Mamet's characters inhabit.

Mixed Blood acquired the rights to *Glengarry Glen Ross*, the Pulitzer winner in 1984, a play about five Chicago real estate salesmen who live or die based on their ability to sell land that people neither need nor want. I had seen the play in Chicago, with Peter Falk and Joe Mantegna in the lead roles of Shelly and Roma. It was electric. The language was pure Mamet, reflecting his vision of America's necrotic heart. When I left the theater that night, I was pumped. When I got back to my hotel, I couldn't sleep. I had seen theater that was truthful, brutal, and memorable—theater that revealed the scabrous underbelly of a caustic body politic. I loved it.

Out of the blue, I got a call from a talented director I'd worked with in a couple of shows, Michael Arndt, who'd been tasked to direct *Glengarry* at Mixed Blood. He wanted to know if I'd do Richard Roma, the pivotal role played by Joe Mantegna in the Chicago production and eventually by Al Pacino in the movie version.

I said simply, "When do we start?" I couldn't believe my luck. A play I loved, a character I was sure I could credibly bring to life, a director I knew and trusted, a theater I considered my home. A grand slam.

Avaricious hucksters just doing business in *Glengarry Glen Ross,*
Mixed Blood Theatre, '86.

I played the role of my life, surrounded by a stellar Mixed Blood veteran cast, spewing Mamet dialogue that thirty years earlier would have earned me a trip to the woodshed and a half-dozen strokes across my butt from Dad's leather belt. But I was bringing to life a character who faithfully revealed Mamet's vision of a cutthroat business as a metaphor for the American waltz with the lure of success. And I was relieved to be able to hit the right notes.

Carla Waldemar of *The Reader* wrote, "Sieve is repugnantly captivating as the loathsomely self-assured, hard-as-nails, amoral snake of a super-salesman who sets up and bilks a poor Joe out of his down payment in Act One and superciliously chews out and undercuts his colleagues in the second act."

Peter Vaughan, in the *StarTribune,* wrote, "Sieve is repellingly brilliant as Roma, who works his magic on an unsuspecting sucker in a wonderful first act scene. He is oily, self-assured, and completely in touch with this rat."

Repugnantly captivating and repellingly brilliant! I want those words on my tombstone.

Actors often say they never read reviews. Not true. They read everything written about them, every time, every opening, every word. An actor's ego will not allow him to ignore even the slightest whiff of faint praise.

My next opportunity to play in the Mamet sandbox came a couple of years later at Mixed Blood when they staged *Speed the Plow,* his brutal satire on Hollywood. The play is a savage study of male panic and the denial of redemptive grace. It's a script filled with opportunities for bravura and high-octane acting. The play dealt with a sense of the ultimate hollowness of an industry and a society based on buddy-buddy values.

Speed the Plow with Joe Minjares and Lia Rivamonte,
Mixed Blood Theatre, '88.

Once again I was offered the Mantegna role, playing Hollywood producer Bobby Gould. The play is an actor's dream, crammed with wonderful, dazzling lines, the message—delivered through the hectic, often overlapping dialogue—was that language is a form of camouflage rather than a means of communication. What you smelled in Mamet's play was the terror and fear that drives a homosocial world like Hollywood and, by implication, that of American capitalism at large. Once again, the critics were kind. I told my friend Joe Minjares at one point during the run that if all I did in the theater for the rest of my life was Mamet, it would be enough.

Oddly, in light of my relatively newfound love of Mamet dialogue and themes and characters, it would be over twenty years before I stepped into another Mamet role, this time in *American Buffalo* as Donny the junk shop owner. In the interim, I'd have the chance to do a Mamet satire, which turned out to be one unforgettably hilarious trip around Mamet's brutal world, accompanied by some of my best friends and actors.

Within a few years of its crackling production of *Speed the Plow*, Mixed Blood presented a little-known script by Arthur Kopit entitled *Road to Nirvana*, a satirical takedown of *Speed the Plow* and the whole Mamet genre of cruel male-bonding rituals with page after page of profane and extremely funny dialogue.

Jack thought it would be a great idea to have the male leads from *Speed the Plow* perform the similar leads in *Road to Nirvana*.

Joe and I were enlisted for what became one of the grossest and funniest productions I ever got myself into.

Twin Cities' theater reviewer, Tad Simons of the *Twin Cities Reader,* wrote, after seeing this production: "You know you've made it as an artist when people start satirizing you. *Road to Nirvana* unites the film producers from *Speed the Plow* five years after they almost killed each other in a previous film deal. The first act of this play is a comic gem. Minjares' character is a coked-up ball of profane energy who spits out Mamet-speak lines such as 'Ya gotta be able to say fuck you, or you're fucked, and that's the fuckin' truth!' as if he were born cursing. As Jerry, Sieve is more low-key and pragmatic, but he wants in on the movie deal so badly that he reluctantly agrees to perform a series of ritual sacrifices cooked up by Al and his girlfriend. Suffice to say that the last scene of the first act is one of the grossest, funniest bits I have ever seen. *Road to Nirvana* is one of the funniest plays to come around in a long time, and Mamet fans will savor the fun had at his expense."

There is no polite way to describe the scene at the end of the first act that Simons is referencing, other than to tell you that it was in keeping with the ethos of virtually every Mamet character that requires them to do *whatever it takes* to close the deal.

Oh, what the hell, it's too good, I have to tell you. If you're queasy or easily upset, just skip to the next page.

In the final scene of the first act, Jerry has to decide whether or not he will eat a spoonful of human excrement solemnly presented to him by his friend Al as a sign that he's all in on the project.

I have no memory of what materials the Mixed Blood Prop Department used to prepare the fake dooky that Joe Minjares gleefully put in front of my face every night during the run of *Road to Nirvana*. And I didn't ask. It smelled vaguely like oatmeal, but looked remarkably like what it was actually supposed to be: a dollop of poop.

It was—how can I say this?—a delicious moment every night as the audience gasped aloud in unison at the precise second, just before the blackout, that I made my decision and opened my mouth to close the deal.

On the final night of the run, it was all Joe and I could do to keep it together as we looked down at the grotesque hors d'oeuvres and saw that the prop master had added a lovely touch to the critical dish: a few small but obvious niblets of corn.

A better takedown of the Mamet view of American commerce could not have been written, a system that turns well-meaning men and women into servants of avarice, and in this case, literally willing to eat shit for the right price. They know what they've become and are willing to pay that price. A line from *Speed the Plow* was our mantra throughout the run of *Road to Nirvana,* when Bobby says to Charlie, "I'm a whore, but I'm a secure whore."

Mixed Blood was on a roll in the early nineties. Somehow Jack got the rights to the latest New York hot property before any other producer in town, and those of us with a strong connection to his theater were in the front row at auditions for these shows.

14

A BRILLIANT TURD

The following season, I got the opportunity to do one of the leads in *Six Degrees of Separation.* Based on the true story of an elaborate con, *Six Degrees* depicts a young black man who claims to be both a friend of a family's Ivy League children and the son of Sidney Poitier. He gains access to their lives by learning about and manipulating their vanity. It's a play about believing, lying, storytelling, art and artifice, and got me one of the more quotable reviews I ever read.

The *City Pages* reviewer Hans Eisenbeis wrote, "Mark Sieve as Flan Kettridge is a brilliant turd, a self-assured mockery of himself and the world he inhabits. He is smooth, cunning, and essentially vapid; a man who has created a veneer as pleasing as one of his prized paintings."

In those quiet moments of self-reflection that happen more and more as I get older, this review occasionally flashes through my head, and if I listen carefully, I can hear the cosmic laughter that tells me that life, if we're not extremely careful, *will* imitate art.

'Six Degrees of Separation' at the Mixed Blood Theatre is marked by solid characterizations from, left to right, Wareen C. Bowles, Marquetta Senters, Mark Sieve and Marie Mathay.

❧

Times come in an actor's progress when he grabs a small role in a play just to work with people who are worth spending eight weeks in their company. I got a call from Jack asking if I wanted to play the role of college maintenance man in a production of *Spinning Into Butter*.

The role was tiny, just a few lines, entrances, and exits throughout the play, with a critical scene toward the end where he has an important conversation with the main character. The bait: three of the Twin Cities most-accomplished veteran actors were involved, and I'd get to hang out with them and see them work: Allen Hamilton, Sally Wingert, and Peter Moore. I'd been watching and appreciating all of them for years.

I said "hell yes" and went to work growing a beard for the maintenance man. It was a rollicking good time, a tight little play about a racial incident at a private Eastern college that asks audiences to confront their own racial attitudes. It involved a Vermont college administrator, played by Sally in a Tony-Award-caliber performance, who must address an incident in which a black student has allegedly been victimized by hate correspondence and vandalism.

We opened at Mixed Blood and moved the show to Park Square in St. Paul to continue its run at the invitation of Park Square as a co-production with Mixed Blood. When the pipes broke and flooded Park Square, we moved it to the Ordway. Every night the dressing room became an arena where Peter and I competed to determine who could make Allen laugh the loudest and longest with the best story.

Mr. Hamilton's gigantic, stentorian laugh was well known, and we worked constantly to see if we could come up with a joke or story he hadn't heard. I'd been doing plenty of comedy with the Puke & Snot Show, but I was pressed to keep up.

The story I remember getting the loudest, longest laugh of the entire run concerned two ancient British explorers reminiscing at the Club. One of them says, "Yes, I'll never forget being on safari in darkest Africa. I was hunting lions late one afternoon, moving stealthily through the dim light, my gun at the ready. Suddenly a lion leaped out at me without warning, *RAAHHRRER!* I crapped my pants."

The other gentleman says sympathetically, "Well, I imagine you would if a lion surprised you like that."

And the first explorer says, "No, just now, when I went *RAAHHRRER!*"

It was a lovely run with lovely people, the kind of show that you recall fondly in your twilight years. Now excuse me, I have to put on some tea and get my slippers, my *Murder She Wrote* reruns are on tonight. That Angela Lansbury is a fox.

The early 2000s was a time for mature roles that tested my experience and abilities. I sunk my teeth into many fine shows at excellent venues with top-notch directors. I got a call again from Jack to audition for his annual bilingual production in which he used English-speaking and Spanish-speaking casts doing the same play, alternating evenings throughout the run.

I was doing a corporate show in Florida at the time and told him I couldn't make the audition. He asked me to put something on tape and send it to the director.

It was an odd request, I'd never been asked to submit a taped audition, but I had a camera and equipment on site in Orlando, laid down a five-minute audition, and sent it out. Amazingly, I got a call three days later asking me to do the role. The play was *Ten Percent of Marta Solano*, a black comedy that gave me a chance to do eight roles—all in the same suit with no costume changes.

The play concerns Marta, a headstrong and confident artist who wants nothing more than to have her driver's license reflect her correct address. She starts at the DMV and runs into a brick wall, via the know-it-all middle-aged bureaucrat who suggests that the easiest solution would be to move to a new address.

Marta sticks to her guns, and the paperwork is filled out for a new license. This simple act cascades. Instead of getting a new license, Marta is declared dead. Her obit runs in the paper, her bank forecloses on her mortgage, and her agent refuses to release any of her money.

At each stop, she is tormented by the same gray middle-aged man, taking on different guises but remaining the same soulless, paper-pushing public servant. Through it all, Marta is never crushed and remains always optimistic, even when she finds herself on death row about to be executed by her longtime tormentor.

It was a mind-bending challenge to play the DMV clerk, a banker, a newspaper publisher, her agent, her mother, a seventy-five-year-old African American President of the United States, her executioner—and to make each character the same yet clearly different. I got to work with one of the best directors I'd ever met, Mark Valdez, who came from Los Angeles and has since often directed at Mixed Blood, in New York, and Los Angeles. He guided me carefully and skillfully through this multi-character test to bring me out successfully on the other side.

Graydon Royce, in the *StarTribune,* wrote, "Sieve is a master at playing the changing bureaucrat with an unchanging message. He keeps it droll and dust dry, never begging for a laugh. As a result, he gets lots of them."

Ten Percent of Marta Solano was one of those shows that persuades the doubting actor mind that, yes, you can do just about anything. Except sing and dance. That you cannot do. I had a knee replacement for God's sake, give me a break.

15

A SMALL BITE OF
THE BIG APPLE

By this time, well into my sixties, I had just about given up on ever getting to Oz, that ultimate actor's destination: New York City. To work in New York, you have to be there pounding the pavement, going to auditions, being rejected, sleeping on other people's sofas, eating Campbell's soup and lots of ramen.

I had many friends over the years who told me all about their journeys in search of that one good break. Some were patient and eventually rewarded. Most weren't. An old friend, Celia Weston, spent five years doing waitress work in Manhattan and performing in free showcases. When she finally got her break in a Broadway show, she quickly picked up a recurring role on an ABC daytime soap opera, and shortly thereafter joined the cast of the CBS sitcom *Alice* as Jolene Hunnicutt until the series ended in 1985. She later appeared in *Dead Man Walking* opposite Susan Sarandon. To date she has had a long career in movies and television, complete with a Tony nomination.

Celia's companion, my old friend "West Virginia Ray" from our Theatre L'Homme Dieu days, was working at Joseph Papp's Public Theater and asked me to come see him in a production of *Henry V*. He told me to watch the actor playing the French queen. He said that, even though she was young and new to New York, she was the best thing in the show.

I went to see Ray play the Duke of Gloucester on a beautiful summer night in Central Park, and I got an unexpected bonus. I saw Meryl Streep dominate the play in the small but critical role of Catherine, the French queen.

Catherine speaks little English, but even right out of college, Streep was a master of dialects. She was captivating. This was the first of dozens of show-stopping stage and film performances from arguably the best actor of our generation.

Ray had been working at some terrific theaters since the infamous Summer of the Birthday Girl. I visited him at the Seattle Repertory Theatre to see a production of *Hamlet* that starred a young actor who was doing an unusual but compelling New York street version of the Danish prince. Christopher Walken would go on to bigger and better roles in bigger and better venues, but that night he was just an up-and-coming stage actor in Seattle.

I knew it was possible, that lightning could strike and literally change your life as an actor. But not unless you put in the time.

I had never set New York as a destination for my acting career. I'd done a ton of good theater with good people and was content with that. But luck had always been a major component of my life, and it was about to make another timely appearance.

The defining year was 2009. I wrote my first book *Call Me Puke* after the death of my longtime comedy partner, Joe Kudla, and it was nearly ready to publish in early spring. I was busy trying to write new material for my new Puke & Snot partner, John Gamoke, who had encouraged me to write the book. My mind was occupied with a thousand things—commerce, comedy, selling my book, running my small production company.

Beyond my regular seasonal Renaissance festival appearances in Colorado, Minnesota, and Maryland, I hadn't stepped on a stage in a theatrical role for several years. Being Puke was enough. I was grateful that after thirty-five years, audiences were still showing up—whether to show their children the Renaissance museum relics known as Puke & Snot or to actually enjoy the comedy, I didn't care.

Festival owners had their reasons for hiring us, and I wasn't arguing. The work wasn't that difficult—four or five shows a day, weekends, with five days off to sleep, read, and play golf. Not a bad gig for a guy in his mid-sixties.

I had a new partner who had injected some needed life into the show with his unique perspective and imposing presence. John had become a popular Snot. Most of my college friends were retired or sitting in boardrooms or spending winters in Palm Desert. I was still doing enough creative work on our show to keep my mind alive. It felt right to keep it rolling. It gave me the motivation to stay in relatively good shape, biking around the Minneapolis lakes, working out at the Y. And once again, Mixed Blood called.

They had scheduled a play by the prestigious playwright, Carlyle Brown, called *Pure Confidence,* to be directed by Marion McClinton, a gifted Tony-nominated director who had directed many of August Wilson's plays on Broadway.

Marion was a St. Paul product. He had worked with my old comedy partner, Joe Kudla, in a production at Theatre in the Round back in the day, and had since risen in the ranks to become one of the best directors in the nation. Marion had already cast several actors I knew but never had the chance to work with: Chris Mulkey, his wife Karen Landry, the outrageously talented Regina Williams, and Gavin Lawrence, a solid actor I had never met but had been doing the lead in this play all over the country for several years.

I was asked if I wanted to play a double role, a Southern plantation owner in the first act and a Northern hotel clerk in the second act. I didn't need to audition; Marion had asked for me.

I thought that a bit odd, I didn't know Marion well, but was aware of his work at Penumbra in St. Paul and around the country, directing Wilson's plays. I knew that Chris Mulkey had been in L.A. doing movies and television. His wife Karen had been a well-known and wonderful stage presence in the Twin Cities since her college days at the U of M. Regina was an actor every director wanted in his cast; she could do anything.

I would be sharing a stage with these talents under the guidance of the best director I would likely ever work with. *Hmm. . .* I thought about it for five seconds and said to Jack, "I'm in."

That began an adventure that, if I never step onstage in another role again in my life, will suffice as a perfectly satisfying end to a long and blessed run in the theater. Carlyle Brown is an award-winning playwright who had come out of the Playwright's Center in Minneapolis, won commissions from the Alabama Shakespeare Festival and the Children's Theatre Company, and was an alumnus of the New Dramatists of New York. He was also a recent Guggenheim Fellow.

His play, *Pure Confidence*, is an intriguing story of an African American jockey, Simon Cato, riding to earn his freedom in the pre-Civil War South. I learned early in rehearsal, thanks to Marion's professorial pre-rehearsal talks, that horse racing in the South before the Civil War was similar to the NBA today. The players—jockeys—were coveted for their ability to win races, and were often sold or traded to other owners who wanted to improve their status on the southern racing circuit.

The story was historically accurate, in that the slave Simon Cato actually sought to buy his freedom using his talents as the best jockey of his era. He fights his "master," social customs, and the law; and the play deals honestly with what it means to own one self—in every sense of the word. I was thrilled to be involved.

At a break in one of our first rehearsals, I asked Marion why he'd asked for me without an audition. It seemed to me that a lot of other actors could have done these two roles. He said simply, "I saw *Glengarry*."

That had been eighteen years previous. I thanked him, went back to rehearsal and silently thanked Mamet for writing that play and giving actors like me a chance to do a role that people remembered.

We opened to excellent reviews, Rohan Preston of the *StarTribune* in Minneapolis called it "a sublime production." The *City Pages* reviewer said, "The play evokes the era of slavery and its aftermath with insight, subtlety, and a thorough respect for the lives it depicts."

I survived my preview night's step off the stage in the blackout with no more than a sore back and a couple of bruises. The ghost light was installed immediately.

As *Pure Confidence* was about to close, Jack mentioned to me that he had been approached by the producers of an Off Broadway theater to bring the play, cast intact, to New York for its America's Off Broadway Festival. The theater, 59E59, combed the country, looking for representative American productions that would look good on its three stages and attract New York audiences. They did the same for their Brits Off Broadway Festival. They had seen our show and wanted it. Jack wasn't interested. "The expense would be horrendous," he explained. They weren't offering anything to defray the costs of shipping sets, paying actors, hiring lighting designers, and stage managers, all of which would be doubly expensive in New York. We closed the show and nobody gave it another thought. Until Jack's email arrived a month later asking us to come to a meeting at the theater.

George DeWitt, slave owner, *Pure Confidence,*
Mixed Blood Theatre and 59E59 Off Broadway, 2009.

The Clerk, *Pure Confidence*

The producers at 59E59 had apparently been relentless. Jack had remained insistent that it couldn't happen unless they came up with some money. They finally called and said, "We'll give you a budget, we want that play on our stage."

The meeting at Mixed Blood was brief. Jack told us what he had to spend. We'd all have to find our own accommodations in the most-expensive city in the country, and it would be a six-week run with a flat salary and no expense allowance. The cast was all in.

I did some mental math and realized that with a little luck and planning, I could become, for a short time, a New York actor in a beautiful production that had already proved itself worthy of a wider audience. And just about break even doing it.

Everybody else was already finding out which New York friend's apartments had sofas that could be rented from late May to early July. I told Jack that if we did this, I'd have to leave the play early to get to my first weekend at the Colorado Renaissance Festival. He said he'd already cast my replacement and that he wanted me to open it and stay as long as I could.

I called my son Pete, who had stayed in Brooklyn recently on a tour with his band, Rogue Valley. He gave me a number in Brooklyn, a guy named Jimmy who rented out his studio apartment in Park Slope to itinerant actors and musicians like us. It was a block from the subway. Perfect. Pete *knew a guy*. I was feeling like a New Yorker before I even arrived.

I called Jimmy that night and Pete's guy came through for me, with a price that coincidentally hit the exact number I had arrived at as a housing allowance for this adventure. Plus $500. But who's counting? And so it went down. I was to become—late in my life but so what?—a New York actor.

If you spend any amount of time around actors and theater people, the conversation eventually turns to New York and L.A. Those are the destinations, the shining cities on their respective hills, the brass rings of the professional actor who hopes against hope to see his name in the closing credits of a good movie or on the marquee outside a New York theater.

The odds are long. It always feels like a classic case of "the grass is greener," no matter how successful you are in Minneapolis, Chicago, or Lincoln, Nebraska. If you want fame and if you want to make a good living in this business, you have to set your sights early on New York or California and get out there. To either one, it makes no difference. You have to get in the mix, get seen, make the connections, hang out in the right theater bars, luck into the right project at the right time.

An old friend in the Twin Cities acting community once told me why he came back to Minneapolis from L.A. after only a year in California trying to break into the film business. He said he rarely went to an audition where the casting director (or an assistant who was screening people for the audition) wasn't a twenty-two-year-old model who couldn't pronounce his name and thought it was "cute" that he'd played "Henry Vee" in Shakespeare's play of the same name. He finally couldn't take it anymore and came back where he knew that, although he'd never become famous, he stood a good chance of making a decent living doing solid work at respected theaters.

I was under no illusion that my impending exposure on a New York stage would bring me anything other than the satisfaction of having done it. Maybe something I could drop into a casual conversation with other actors over a bourbon that might help establish some credibility that I was one of them; I belonged.

The actor ego is a fragile thing. Acceptance is a big deal. Working in New York or L.A. is like making your bones in the mob; you're not taken seriously until you've done the hard work and either knocked off somebody from another family or got cast in the 34th revival of *Hair*.

Our tight-knit little cast of *Pure Confidence* was gung-ho from the start. We all arrived on 59th Street in New York determined to dominate *The New York Times* Entertainment section when we opened our proven little show.

Regina couldn't make the trip with us because of a previous casting commitment at the Guthrie Theater; but her replacement, Christiana Clark, a graceful and talented choice, fit in immediately. Otherwise, we were all there. And all the little goose-bumpy things about being in a New York show began revealing themselves as soon as we arrived at the theater for the first rehearsal. Our names were on the dressing room door—preceded by "Mr." or "Miss." A large hanging sign outside the theater had our names prominently displayed. Gorgeous marketing posters popped up in the lobby window cases. The stage manager and her assistant checked in constantly to see if we needed anything, anything at all. The daily laundering of costumes felt like someone was paying close attention to everything, even our socks. Then there were the teaser articles in the New York papers and magazines. Truly, I thought at the time, I would have done this for nothing (not something an actor *ever* tells a producer, but it was how I felt).

The daily subway rides from Brooklyn to Manhattan and back, the visits to the marvelous deli down the block from Jimmy's studio apartment, renting a bike and riding around Prospect Park on sunny spring days, hanging out in Central Park people-watching with my son Pete who flew in to spend a few days and see the show, each

New York moment became part of a singular and gratifying total immersion experience for this aging Midwestern boy, in its own way a perfect coda to my forty years of dabbling in the theater world.

We opened perfectly. The play was well-received, eventually winning three Audelco Awards for best actor (Gavin), best director (Marion), and best lighting design (Andy Mayer).

New York reviewer John Simon was especially pleased, writing, "The Mixed Blood Theatre of Minneapolis has brought *Pure Confidence* to the 59E59 Theaters complex in Manhattan, and this unheralded work deserves your attention . . . [Carlyle] Brown has come up with a fascinating story, racy characters and salty dialogue. Marion McClinton, astute director of several August Wilson plays, does as handsomely by Brown's tale. He's chosen an exemplary cast, in which even supporting roles are strongly taken by Mark Sieve and Casey Greig. Chris Mulkey and Karen Landry are compelling as the Johnsons, and Gavin Lawrence is all vim and vigor as Simon. And even more astounding is the performance of Caroline by Christiana Clark, which grows to staggering power as if in a time exposure. It all adds up to a finely conceived slice of Americana, providing a pungent history lesson blessedly devoid of dryness or preachment."

The New York Times reviewer also had some nice things to say: "The veteran director Marion McClinton makes the production a theatrical sure thing. He knows when to slow the drama and when to pump it up, and he stages the action scenes cleverly and simply, using movement, light and imagination. The audience eats it up. There were tears during Mattie and Caroline's reunion, and a standing ovation at the end."

Pure Confidence cast with Karen, Chris, Casey,
Gavin, Christiana, and Julia the stage manager.

A *CurtainUp* reviewer wrote: "Mark Sieve's convincing dual portrayals of arrogant Southern slave-owner George DeWitt, and later the bigoted Saratoga, New York, hotel clerk, neatly reveal national attitudes at the time."

I'm going to have those reviews framed and hung on my basement rec room wall. I was in good company and loving every moment. Leaving this show early would be difficult. Traveling to the theater on the F train every night from Brooklyn and going back later that night in the company of the usual New York cast of subway characters had become a routine I could see myself doing for the next six months or more.

But as the time came for me to get back to Minnesota and pack my tights, puffy shirts, swords, and vegetables for another summer in the mountains of Colorado, I resolved to at least finish this memorable run without falling off the stage in the first act blackout. That I accomplished.

I said goodbye to some of the best people I'd ever shared the stage lights with and left for home, knowing well that it was only my usual amazing good fortune that had allowed me to tack an unexpected exclamation point onto my theatrical history. I would likely never come this way again.

Except I did, in 2015—to watch my kid on Letterman.

I got a call from my son Pete, who let me know as calmly as he could that he'd be playing lead guitar and singing with the Jeremy Messersmith Band on *Late Night with David Letterman* later that spring.

Pete is an accomplished musician, a member of one of the best Americana folk/rock bands I've had the privilege to follow for many years, Rogue Valley. Like a lot of musicians in the Twin Cities, Pete plays with other bands when they need him. They all know each other and, with a few days of rehearsals, are often interchangeable. Jeremy needed Pete to fill in for his lead guitarist on his latest tour.

Messersmith is a compelling songwriter and performer whose latest album, *Heart Murmurs,* caught the ear of the Letterman producers, and they'd booked him for an appearance. Pete agreed to join him.

When I put down the phone, I went to my laptop and

immediately got a flight and a hotel room. Pete showed up for me when I made my New York debut. I was not going to miss this chance to see my kid play and sing on my favorite late-night talk show.

Pete's older brother Pat is also an accomplished guitarist in the mode of a Stevie Ray Vaughan bluesman and an eighties' hair band shredder. I'm sure Pete's admiration of his brother's skills was one of the driving forces that led him to become the artist he is today. They're both topnotch guitarists, and this was Pete's opportunity to do what few players get to do—the guest band slot on Dave's show.

Pete got me a backstage pass. I showed up at the theater, hung out with Paul Shaffer and the band, watched Dave skulk through the hallways, and sat through rehearsals with Biff mispronouncing Messersmith several times.

Finally I heard Jeremy and his band, along with a string quartet, absolutely kill the assembled full house with a beautiful rendition of *Bubblin'*, a gorgeous song from his new album. Look it up on YouTube, *Jeremy Messersmith on Letterman,* it's a fantastic performance.

Proud of my kid.

Pete (in the white tee) with the Jeremy Messersmith Band
on the *Late Show with Letterman,* 2015.

16

EFFIN RUTHIE

Two years after my spiritual and theatrical pilgrimage to New York, my old Mixed Blood buddy, Pat O'Brien, came to me with an idea. He'd been touring his one-man show at fringe festivals around the country, but wanted to do a small-cast play, one that we could afford to produce by paying two or three actors (mainly ourselves) and one that was written to be performed on a single set with basic lighting and simple props. Was I interested?

Yeah. Did he have a play in mind? Yes.

Pat always wanted to play Teach, the violent and unstable seminal character in Mamet's award-winning play *American Buffalo*, originally performed by Al Pacino in New York and eventually in the movie. There was a good role in it for me, a junk shop owner friend of Teach named Don.

We went bowling one Sunday morning with Jack and talked about the possibilities. Jack had a month in the middle of winter where Mixed Blood was dark. He would rent the theater to us. Patrick brought a copy of the play. An early scene in *American Buffalo* immediately identified the play as a Mamet original:

[SCENE   Don's shop, Don is at the counter behind his cash register. Teach enters]

TEACH   Fuckin Ruthie, fuckin Ruthie, fuckin Ruthie, fuckin Ruthie, fuckin Ruthie!

I recognized the elegant Mamet voice. I was in.

We needed a third actor to play the boy, and we needed a director. Pat convinced me that we could save money and direct it ourselves. He even quoted Mamet's opinion of directors as "unnecessary, all they do is fuck up a good play." If Mamet said that, who was I to disagree? We were experienced actors and directors; we could manage a simple three-actor play.

Even with a small marketing budget, we'd be able to showcase our talents at a respected Twin Cities venue. We put together a basic budget, hired a set designer, and started rehearsals.

Things were moving along on schedule; I was relishing once again spitting out Mamet's biting dialogue, our small three-man cast was solving movement and motivation problems nicely. But one memorable—some would say predictable—day, halfway through the rehearsal process, a huge argument broke out over a relatively simple piece of stage business.

The kid was sitting in the shop while Don and Teach were arguing. The actor playing the kid reached over and picked up a magazine while Don was making a major point. I stopped.

ME   What are you doing?

ACTOR   I think he might decide to read a little while you two are arguing.

ME   Why would he do that?

ACTOR   Maybe he's heard all this before and he's bored.

ME   They're arguing about something that could cost you your life, I'm pretty sure you'd be paying attention.

ACTOR   I don't think so.

ME   You don't think [GROWING FRUSTRATED] Pat, what do you think?

PATRICK   Yeah, I think he might pick up the magazine.

ME   You think he—really?

PATRICK   Yeah.

ME   No! All that does is create an action that takes the focus off the main point of our argument; he *can't* pick up that magazine and drop out of the scene.

PATRICK   It's an interesting choice. He might do that, yes.

ME   You can't be serious. I totally disagree. Any action that distracts from the dialogue you and I are having is a mistake. It's absolutely the wrong thing to do.

PATRICK   I don't think so.

ACTOR   I think it's a good choice.

ME   Let's take a ten-minute break.

I stomped out to find a place to cool off. As I went by Jack's office, he was sitting at his desk, smiling. He had heard our tense little discussion and offered his small but noteworthy observation: "There's a reason the director's name is in large print in the program."

I licked my wounds and decided to yield. There would be more important battles to fight before we got this play onstage.

But lesson learned. I'll never self-direct another play, it's like NBA basketball with no referees. Doesn't work. Mamet is full of crap; directors are critical. Without them, actors will waste hours of rehearsal time massaging their egos and arguing about nonsense a director would solve with a quick decision.

We opened the show on schedule, attracting small crowds of curious Mamet fans over a short, artistically satisfying two-week run. It was another rewarding Mamet adventure for me, reminding me what I'd been missing since my last go round.

Fuckin Mamet, fuckin Mamet, fuckin Mamet . . .

❧

Patrick and I had enough fun with *American Buffalo* to start looking for another show we could do together. Pat found a tasty little script called *Rounding Third*, a two-character play about the terrors and rewards of fathers managing their kids in Little League baseball.

I played Don (again), a Vince Lombardi-style, win-at-all-costs, take-no-prisoners blue collar manager whose son was the team's star pitcher. Pat played the corporate executive dad, Michael, always tied to his cellphone, who agrees to be Don's assistant because he wants to share an activity with his son who's never played the game. He just wants the kids to have fun.

The play is the tumultuous journey of these two Little League coaches through an entire season, from their first tentative meeting to the climactic championship game. The audience is the stand-in for the team, so the coaches speak directly to the audience about competition, character, punctuality, and the importance of wearing the right equipment. And over the course of exhilarating victories, heartbreaking defeats, and interminable rainouts, the two men battle over how to lead the team.

Out of their conflicting philosophies, the real issues of the play emerge: how should we raise our children? Since we live in such a ferociously competitive society, do we protect our children as long as possible? Or do we prepare them to be tough enough to win? And what does it mean to be an American man?

By the end of the play, Don's personal life has come crashing down around him, and he's forced to see both his son and the team in a different light. And Michael must confront an unfamiliar but powerful sensation: he *really* wants to win.

This time we hired a good friend and an experienced director, Mark Bergren, to guide us. That decision turned out to be a wise one.

Jack was correct, we should have put Mark's name in lights outside. But there were difficulties. The first obstacle to surmount: I was nearing seventy years old, and Patrick was trying to catch up. We were both a little long in the tooth to be playing Little League coaches with kids on the team; but hell, that's what makeup and proper lighting are for. Besides, we thought, if we weren't good enough by now to make people forget little things like how old we were, then our whole careers had been for naught.

How old was Mary Martin when she did Peter Pan? See? And both of us had coached our own sons in youth baseball, so the material was familiar, there was nothing mysterious about the script.

So we hired an experienced set painter who created a gorgeous hand-painted Little League field, we hung it as our backdrop, plunked down a bench and went to work at the Bryant Lake Bowl, a combination theater, restaurant and bowling alley in South Minneapolis that had a reputation for hosting odd variety and theatrical events. A million miles from Off Broadway, it was basic theater, but all we needed. We had no marketing budget and produced this little epic in the middle of winter in Minnesota, so the crowds were sparse.

No official reviewers showed up, but the best review we got was from my brother Kurt, like me, a former baseball player. His laughter throughout the show in all the right spots told me what I needed to know about the ultimate impact of the show.

By the time we closed a couple of weeks later, the actors were still both standing. A triumph.

The standing part, I mean.

They say when life gives you lemons, make lemonade. Lemons? I wish. Life has handed me an abundance of nose hair and a bad prostate—but also an uncanny knack for being in the right place at the right time.

Rounding Third was a chance for Pat O'Brien and me to indulge our not-so-secret love of the national pastime and trot around in the stage lights while we did it. A couple of years later, the aforementioned Jack Reuler, also a big baseball fan, told us on one of our Sunday morning bowling outings that he'd found a script about baseball that he wanted to stage at a ballpark. The catch was that the audience would move from scene to scene while the actors stayed in one place and repeated their scenes for each new group of audience members that came through.

The marvelous Pat O'Brien and me, coaching our asses off,
Rounding Third, Bryant Lake Bowl, 2016.

Pat and I aren't the sharpest knives in the drawer—well, he is—but we had a hard time getting our heads around exactly how that idea might work. Jack patiently explained that the play was written in nine scenes, no actor appearing in more than one, the scenes were written to be staged in offices, locker rooms, hallways, kitchens, rest rooms, concourses, and skyboxes all over a stadium. It concerned a young Latino pitcher for San Diego who *might* be considering staging a protest on the mound at the start of the seventh game of the World Series. And—best of all—there were roles for Pat and me.

Thus the following spring found me in my old double-breasted gray suit, playing a major league director of umpires doing a scene with one of my favorite Twin City actors and friends, Warren Bowles, in the world premiere of *Safe At Home*, produced by Mixed Blood and starring everybody in town and a few flown in from far-off places like L.A. and New York.

The play was a fascinating mix of professional sports, race, white identity politics, immigration, labor-management relations, and the agonizing difficulty of staying true to yourself while continuing to do what you love. In other words, a perfect Mixed Blood play.

The *City Pages* reviewer wrote, "Audiences are in close with these actors, with views of their characters' accustomed surroundings, from the luxury boxes with panoramic views to the long, bare corridor where players wait to enter the dugout like gladiators stepping into an arena. One of the most compelling settings is a windowless batting cage, surreally outfitted with lush green artificial turf. As a major league baseball executive (Mark Sieve) confronts the head umpire (Warren C. Bowles) about the potential player protest, it feels like the curtain is being pulled back on a cloistered brotherhood.

"It's an impressive technical achievement, one that would threaten to overwhelm the drama if the writing wasn't so sharp and the acting wasn't so impressive. Director Reuler has assembled a top notch cast, and it's easy to imagine jumping at the opportunity to be a part of this unique adventure in site-specific theater."

'Safe at Home' uses all the nooks and crannies of CHS Field to create an amazing piece

Thursday, March 9, 2017 by Jay Gabler in
Arts & Leisure

Rich Ryan

Site-specific theater! Warren and I hung "backstage" behind a curtain in the batting cage until the between-scenes music played.

We walked out on cue and engaged in our tense seven-minute confrontation more than a hundred times that week.

Each scene had to be EXACTLY seven minutes, because the music would play and, no matter where you were as an actor in that scene, it was over. The audience moved on with a guide to the next scene in another part of the stadium. We even had a monitor that counted down the final thirty seconds so we could tell if we were running ahead or behind. Running ahead was no problem; a few longer-than-usual dramatic pauses would solve that. But running behind resulted in some speedy line readings that the authors hadn't intended. It was a blast, a brand-new theater experience, and one that all of us simply devoured.

The locker/dressing room before and after each performance was not at all unlike the baseball locker rooms I'd inhabited as a player in college and semi-pro ball, but instead of players and coaches it was actors *playing* players and coaches. Very cool, very real, and it brought a reality to the play and the performances that radiated to the audience.

At this late stage of my actor life, it seemed fitting and fortunate that I'd be offered a play that not only gave me a chance to sink my teeth into a good character role, but to do it in a setting where I'd spent a great part of my younger years working to become—not an actor—but a professional ballplayer. Truly, both the subject matter, the cast, director, and the theater I owed my professional development to made me feel absolutely *Safe At Home.*

17

MAXING OUT

When I took a leave of absence from teaching in the Minneapolis
Public Schools during the winter of 1981, never to return, I threw
myself into any and every acting job that came my way. I did
commercials, corporate videos, modeling work, plays, and emcee
gigs where I had to pretend to understand the corporate culture of
the company that I was handing out awards to.

It was a fair trade-off for my recently abandoned career in
education. I recognized at some point that, contrary to my dad's
advice to his children, "If there's any way you can do it, be your
own boss." I was not only not my own boss, but I was becoming
more aware that if I stayed in teaching until the day they sent me off
with a signed Certificate of Appreciation from the superintendent
and a gift card for a dinner at Applebee's—alone—I'd never be
making my own decisions about my financial future.

The Puke and Snot Show was a reliable weekend gig that Joe

and I had built into an eighteen-to-twenty-five-week enterprise at its peak. During those months when the show overlapped my teaching job I'd been working seven days a week. That was a bit much.

I was confident that if Renaissance festivals didn't suddenly disappear as a uniquely American cultural curiosity, I'd probably be able to make a living. But I still wouldn't truly be my own boss.

In late '88, my agent called and sent me to an audition for a quirky corporate show, where I would be doing a live digitized Max Headroom character for a local Minneapolis producer. You don't remember Max? Max Headroom was a fictional artificial intelligence (AI) character, known for his wit and broken, distorted, electronically sampled voice. He was introduced in early 1984, played by actor Matt Frewer, and became something of a media phenomenon.

Frewer portrayed him as "the world's first computer-generated TV host," although the computer-generated appearance was achieved with prosthetic makeup and hand-drawn backgrounds.

Max was a "computerized" live actor who made a career out of appearing only onscreen, beamed in from some alien digitized world only he understood. The show they wanted me to do would be a knockoff of Frewer's concept. It would be in Chicago, and it paid well. I showed up at the audition, got the job, and we left for Chicago the following week.

The eighties and nineties were a good time for actors doing corporate videos and live appearances. Companies were spending a lot of money to get their sales forces together to party, celebrate the year's successes, and promote the business and marketing plans for the coming year. These national get-togethers needed entertainment, interesting ways to present their ideas to large groups, and talented actors and directors to make these shows as professional as possible.

Matt Frewer as his creation, Max Headroom

The Wilson Learning Company in Minneapolis was churning out two or three educational videos a week in their suburban studios with large casts being paid union rates. I was given the heads up about Wilson from a friend who'd been working there, introduced myself to the directors, and quickly got cast in the first of what were to be dozens of video projects that were shot in English and translated into a wide variety of languages for foreign sales. I had been getting on-the-job training on-camera for some years by then, becoming more and more comfortable each time I stepped into a shot.

The Chicago Max Headroom-style gig was different, requiring improvisation, connecting live with a large audience from a remote location, using sound effects and digital video images to create a whole new video reality. I would be in heavy makeup, sit in a small eight-by-eight foot curtained "studio envelope" backstage, with a camera and engineer in front of me and hot lights three feet away. At the appointed time, I was projected into the adjoining ballroom on the big screen as an over-the-top digitized talking head, asking questions, cracking jokes written for their culture and clients, and generally emceeing the proceedings with the presenters.

I wore sunglasses, purportedly to add mystery to this strange electronic entity, but actually to allow me to read script without the audience seeing my eyes. The engineer performed a series of video tricks to encourage the illusion that the character was overriding the hotel system and beaming in from some rogue computer source.

I had a monitor in front of me so I could hear the dialogue from the speakers and audience in the ballroom, and I was allowed to improvise dialogue as long as I stayed in character and true to my digitized environment. It was bizarre, and it worked. The client was ecstatic, the audience had no idea where this talking head came from or how it was produced.

I did this gig twice more in other cities until the third job, in Toronto, where things got weird. I showed up at the script meeting in a hotel conference room with four of the clients. The producer was strangely uncommunicative and distant. The clients weren't happy with the script and wanted an immediate re-write before rehearsal. The script I had been given was similar in tone and structure to my previous two shows, and I assumed either the producer or his writer would be able to solve this problem forthwith.

We started reading through the script and the VP of Sales asked for a different joke on the second page. We looked at my producer, and he mumbled, "Maybe we could use the time travel joke there . . . excuse me, I have to make a phone call." And he was gone.

All eyes turned to me. Damn. Did I just become the head writer for this thing?

I was now the only person at this meeting from Minneapolis, so yes, there were no apparent options.

"Well," I said, "Let's see what we can come up with here." I began throwing out ideas for script changes that I thought might work based on reactions I'd gotten in my previous two shows. I threw in a few Puke & Snot can't-miss jokes along the way, and in an hour we had a script they were willing to try.

Mr. Time Travel had disappeared, leaving me to become the writer and producer as well as the talent. And as far as I knew, I was still only being paid as the actor.

The rehearsal began, and after a couple of hours of successfully negotiating the technical problems and doing another re-write, it was show time. I hadn't seen a check yet for the first two shows, I was sweaty, and I smelled like duct tape and cheap makeup. I was annoyed, moving toward pissed.

I decided to finish the show as professionally as I could and deal with my frustrations in the clear light of day. I definitely smelled a rat. How do you walk out of a client meeting and leave an actor to solve your script problems?

I decided to meet with my agent as soon as I got back and find out what was going on.

In her office two days later, my agent revealed that the producer was "trying" to pay me and other actors he'd fallen behind with. Other actors? People I knew?

I made some calls. I found out quickly that this producer apparently had been snorting his money up his nose. I wasn't the only other actor in town he'd stiffed.

Now I was angry, moving toward enraged. I called Garth Schumacher, an actor friend I knew had worked with this guy, we got together over coffee and that's when I found out that this doofus owed Garth thousands for jobs going back months. I suddenly realized I was in a long line of people waiting for payment.

Minneapolis isn't a big town; it's hard to do business like that before they find out who you are. Garth and I commiserated. He'd been doing exactly what I'd been asked to do, acting and writing and producing the show for the company. The Nose was getting a three-for-one and not paying for any of it.

I was looking for justice, any way we could collect from this deadbeat that was legal and didn't require doing what we heard another friend of ours had done, which was brilliant but risky (he asked a large actor friend of his to go with him to the Nose's house and stand behind him like Luca Brasi while he waited at the front door for his check).

At some point in our conversation I heard my father's voice—"Be your own boss"—and I said to Garth, "Why don't we produce these characters ourselves? We can do it better and we'll hurt him right in the bank account."

The concept hadn't even been the Nose's idea in the first place. We found out that a local magician had suggested that he try the Max Headroom illusion on one of his corporate clients. He did and the audience never made the connection that they were actually watching a live character on their big screens. They all thought it was somehow ingeniously taped and timed. Magic! And whenever the character would talk directly to someone onstage or in the audience, the effect was electric. It was simple "magical misdirection" done with audio, video, good acting, and imaginative writing.

Garth had done many more of these than I had. He'd written quite a few shows. We both knew a couple of technicians who could put together the equipment we needed. We knew the Nose had been overcharging for this concept, and if we could talk a few clients into hiring us we might be able to build a business that would not only compete with the Nose's company, but make us some decent money along the way.

We went to work designing some basic marketing materials and came up with a name (Custom Interactive Characters Inc, which we quickly shortened to CIC). We started talking to tech friends of ours who could put together the right pieces of video equipment to give us the capability to mount these shows.

Within a week, Garth had some exciting news. He'd gotten a call from the VP of Sales of a company who wanted to hire him to reprise a character he'd done for their last national sales meeting. The Nose had told the VP he couldn't use Garth again but that he'd be glad to send another actor. The VP had then called Garth directly to ask him why he was no longer available.

Garth gave him the right answer. "I have good news and bad news. The bad news is you can't get me through my former company, I don't work his projects any more. The good news is you can hire me through mine, we're producing these interactive characters now."

Garth set up a meeting for the following week.

We were about to make our first sales pitch, with a lot of money on the line. Garth had created the character of The Coach for this company, and the sales reps loved him—a loud, cheerful, motivational, slightly dim but loveable generic coach who arrived at their meeting electronically and was there to fire up the sales force. They wanted a return of their new mascot for their next meeting, and another actor wouldn't cut it. They wanted Garth. We had him, and we had a shot at the show if we could convince them we could produce the technology.

Garth and his electronic characters.

The Nose had convinced his clients that his technology was mysterious and rare, impossible to reproduce, and available only through him. Our job was to get them to trust us that we could do the same show at half the price with complete transparency. We had to convince them that the technology was easily acquired and their former producer had been ripping them off at the prices we knew he was charging.

The clients were overjoyed to see Garth. We made our pitch,

gave them a budget, explained the technology and sat back in our chairs while six men in expensive suits looked at us and fiddled with their pencils.

After a long, tense silence, the VP of Marketing spoke up. "Okay folks, we got The Coach if we want him. Do you trust Garth? He says he can do this, and I think he can. Does anybody at this table have any balls?"

The laughter broke the tension, the VP of Sales stood up and said "Let's do this, I'll get a contract to you tomorrow."

And CIC was off and running. In the best possible way we could have done it, by taking a job from right under the Nose's nose and beginning to pay ourselves back with money that would have gone up his Nose.

Garth and I were about to become our own bosses.

That job put us on the map as legitimate producers, and our next job served up even-sweeter just desserts. The Dayton-Hudson Company needed an interactive character for the second-floor video wall in their downtown Minneapolis store over the Christmas season to engage holiday shoppers and chat live with them as they strolled by.

We came up with Digit the Elf. We found out during the negotiations that Dayton's had originally approached the Nose for this project but their legal department told them they couldn't do a contract with his company. His reputation had caught up with him. CIC was the fortunate beneficiary.

We ended up doing two more video wall characters for Valentine's Day and Easter, created some slick marketing materials, and the legend of the Little Company That Could grew apace.

We did shows all over the country, creating custom-designed big screen characters for meetings large and small. Elvis, the

Hamm's Beer bear, Greek Gods, robots, elves, the Easter Bunny, an NBA Draft character, a Minnesota Vikings Award show, Disney, and superheroes for every industry imaginable. We even brought Ronald Reagan back to life on the big screen at a meeting where his old Chief of Staff Alexander Haig was the keynote speaker.

And we were able to do all of this simply because some clown thought he could get by with not paying his actors. There's a lesson in there somewhere. I have no idea what it is. But the lesson Garth and I learned by starting our own business was that the only difference between bravery and stupidity is whether or not you're successful.

W. D. Gigs, a character for a Disney Company meeting in Orlando.

THE ART OF
PLANNED SURPRISE.

The deadlier the topic, the more of a life saver we are.

PLANNED SURPRISE #1. THIS LOOKS LIKE A COMPUTER GENERATED CHARACTER. BUT IT'S LIVE AND RESPONDS TO YOUR PEOPLE.

If you've ever seen Max Headroom, you know the look of the characters that we create for you.

So the look gets them to expect one thing, then we show them another.

Like when someone sneezes and our character says "gesundheit."

PLANNED SURPRISE #2. IT LOOKS LIKE OUR CHARACTER AD LIBS WITH YOUR PRESENTER. BUT WE PRE-SCRIPT EVERY WORD TO MAKE YOU LOOK GOOD.

The crowd loves it. Then, the dry presenter becomes the juicy one.

And, it's a great way for the boss to be a real person and loved for it.

Let's say character zings the boss. Applause.

Then the boss tops the character with a better zing. Standing ovation.

PLANNED SURPRISE #3. PEOPLE WILL TALK ABOUT THIS FOR YEARS. BUT WHAT THEY SAY WILL BE NICE.

When someone says "do you remember the meeting when..." it's usually about something that went embarrassingly wrong.

Well, our characters are zany enough to get you that kind of attention, too.

The difference: You keep the fascination and lose the embarrassment. So, you end up the winner:

PLANNED SURPRISE #4. WE MAKE THE DULLEST PARTS OF THE MEETING FUN. THIS HELPS WHEN THE NEWS ISN'T ALL GOOD.

What if the sales force can't get enough product? Or the company's just been sold? Or any of a thousand other tough business problems. That's when you need an emotional response from your people and a positive one.

LAUGHTER RELEASES ENDORPHINS FROM THE BRAIN. SO WE'RE AS CLOSE AS YOU'LL GET TO A VIDEO HIGH.

That's why we supply a lot of relief, no matter what your pain. Even if it's the pain of having to get through some terribly dry subject matter without losing your audience. By the time our character finishes, it will be the highlight of the meeting.

"I ain't just blowin' smoke up your hat either, partner."

"Does the ringing in my ears bother you at all?"

"Having trouble finding a date? Lower your standards."

"They're jokes. They're all jokes."

"I'm in big trouble. You management guys are starting to make sense to me."

"Weeeelll. I'm sure I'll remember that just as soon as this meeting's over."

Michael Levin as Digit the Elf with the inside story on Santa for Dayton's video wall.

As the iconic Hamm's Bear.

A CIC show in Las Vegas for—you got it—a hair products company.

With our genius engineer for many years, Dick Kohl.

An interactive robot, Vanguard Max, for ECOLAB.

The CIC ownership team in a production meeting, 1990.

18

MARK. MY WORDS

"It was almost no trick at all, he saw, to turn vice into virtue and slander into truth, impotence into abstinence, arrogance into humility, plunder into philanthropy, thievery into honor, blasphemy into wisdom, brutality into patriotism, and sadism into justice. Anybody could do it; it required no brains at all. It merely required no character."
—Joseph Heller, *Catch 22*

It's 2019. To be perfectly honest, in my humble opinion of course, without offending anyone who thinks differently, from my point of view, but also by looking at this matter with a different perspective and without condemning anyone else's views, and by trying to keep it objective, and by considering each and every one's valid opinion, I honestly believe that I completely forgot what I was going to say.

Wait. Yes. I was talking in the previous chapter about some clown not paying his bills. A deadbeat. A con man. Like someone whose whole life has been dedicated to self-promotion and self-aggrandizement, a liar and a thief, someone who always punches down on the less fortunate, never up at the more powerful. Some Mamet-like creation that far exceeds even the dark vision he would present as the classic American deal-maker prototype, the sociopathic narcissist whose only interest is self-interest, and who understands that America is only too ready at any given time for another newly-adapted production of *The Music Man.*

The first two-plus years of the Trump presidency served up a toxic brew of anger, disbelief, depression, and fury as I lived out in real time with millions of others a radical turn in this country, a tectonic shift from what I thought was a relatively reasonable and empathetic society to an autocratic, dystopian hellscape of racism, lies, denial, misogyny, cruelty, arrogance, and fear.

As I'm pecking away at this epic in late July of 2019, a well-known New York writer, E. Jean Carroll, has accused the President of the United States of raping her two decades ago when she worked across the street from Trump Tower at Bergdorf Goodman. The President's response: "I didn't rape her, she's not my type."

Yes. He said that, prompting a good friend to wonder, "I'm curious as to exactly which type of woman it is that appeals to his rapey side."

This latest brutally detailed and credible accusation adds to at least fifteen other accounts of sexual assaults of fifteen other women by President Donald J. Trump.

And just as we process this startling news, reports surface this same day of hundreds of migrant children being held in appalling and filthy conditions in a detention facility in Clint, Texas, with outbreaks of flu and lice and scabies. Unattended sick two-year-olds are being cared for by seven- and eight-year-olds. Attorneys who witnessed the conditions in the facility likened it to torture, and some said if prisoners of war were treated like this it would be a violation of the Geneva Convention. Seven children have died in detention since Trump instituted his family separation policy at the border, the first children to die in US custody in ten years.

Children are being given one glass of water a day, frozen or barely cooked food, and no soap or toothbrushes. The kids are forced to sleep on cold concrete floors with a single foil "blanket" and no mattresses or pillows. Lights are kept on all night, resulting in even more sleep deprivation.

It is state sanctioned child abuse. It's not merely negligent child abuse; it's being done with purposeful, malicious intent to deter people from coming to our country and seeking asylum—the same asylum we have always offered to oppressed people who come to us from around the world. Offering asylum is a hallmark of this country. Beyond even the damning Mueller Report, the idea that we would undo that American policy by engaging in state-sanctioned child abuse is the clearest indictment yet of this feckless, cruel administration.

And to complete this trifecta of Presidential horrors and provide a bonus subject for my next therapy session: the President of the United States just walked the nation to the brink of war with

Iran, then called it off and bragged that he showed "great leadership." He also announced he'll be staging yet another meeting and photo op with the leader of one of the world's most deadly regimes, Kim Jong Un. His close personal friend. According to our President, they "fell in love."

All in all, just another week in the hellish landscape of a country run by a lawless and corrupt executive branch that answers to no one and respects no law. And it's only Tuesday.

Meanwhile, the nation is still processing the recently released Mueller Report that reads like an investigation of Tony Soprano and his family, with corruption, bribery, and lies leaping off every page. Anyone who bothers to read it, and I have, will see that the contents of the report prepared by former special counsel Robert Mueller do *not* clear Trump of collaborating with Russia to interfere in the 2016 election, and it *absolutely* shows that POTUS acted to obstruct the investigation. It's important stuff, exhausting, damning, and frightening.

As with all things in politics and life, you have to know about it to care about it. Most Americans haven't seen the report; they don't know how strong the evidence is. They're busy working, raising kids, living their lives, trying to survive. Understandable. However, for members of the legislative branch of our government, whose job is to oversee the executive branch, to not read the report (as most senators and congressmen and congresswomen have not), there's no greater proof that those politicians are uninterested in actual facts.

Christ on a bicycle! How did we get here?

❧

John and I were doing a festival in Florida during the 2016 election. Sarasota is a picturesque Gulf Coast community that values education and the arts and has always been one of Florida's most welcoming cities for social and political progressives. It has great golf courses, sparkling beaches, terrific weather, excellent restaurants and nonstop night life. It also has cockroaches, alligators, red tide, snakes, corrupt politicians, humidity, and a generous share of Trump fans.

Katherine Harris was a karaoke hostess here before Jeb Bush named her Secretary of State in 2000, she oversaw the theft of the election for Jeb's brother by throwing thousands of black and Hispanic voters off the rolls using lists of similar names of prison inmates from Texas. Much later I found out with other Americans that the state of Florida threw out one in fifty white votes in that election, and one in nine black votes. That fact alone caused me to look at Florida differently after that.

The sight of red-hatted Trumpers drinking and holding signs on street corners along Highway 41, asking cars to honk if they loved Trump was unsettling, but nothing to lose sleep about. Surely they knew, deep down, he was a con man and a grifter, he had a well-known thirty-plus year history of bankruptcies and stiffing vendors and small businesses. A couple of Google clicks could tell you all you needed to know about his history of racism, lawsuits, and cons large and small. Besides, this was still the South. The rest of the country surely knew these facts. Never did I believe in a million years that this self-promoting charlatan could win a national election.

John and I had tried the Puke & Snot Political Sketch at the festival our first day in Sarasota. The stony silence that greeted those jokes caused us to rethink our approach that day and replace that sketch with the less controversial Robin Hood bit. More hilarity, less hostility. Always the right choice if you're doing comedy.

We wrote it off as an anomaly, it was hot and humid. Florida wasn't Minnesota or Maryland; there were likely to be more conservatives around here whose sense of humor might not align with ours. But that was *comedy*. Surely the country knew the difference between comedy and electoral disaster.

On Tuesday, Election Eve, November 2016, I watched with growing horror as the numbers came in from all over the country. Watching television that night was like having my eyes removed with a potato peeler.

I thought of the bizarre sign over the Houston car dealership that Joe and I had seen for years as we drove our rental car up I-45 to the Texas Renaissance Festival: OWNER HAS BRAIN DAMAGE. That guy sold a lot of cars and was still in business long after we left Texas in the mid-eighties. *Has the whole nation just bought a car from this guy?*

A few lines from our political sketch popped into my head:

PUKE   I am a new breed of politico! In the old days, politicians would pretend to be your friend, only to steal your money, your land, your freedom!

SNOT   And you're different because . . .?

PUKE   I'm not pretending!

On the Wednesday morning following the election, it was clear that the maddening vicissitudes of the Electoral College had once again screwed over the will of the people (See Bush V. Gore, 2000). In fact the whole country was now to be subjected to the narcissistic whims of an admitted sexual predator who ran for election on a five-year campaign to convince voters that their black President was illegitimate because somehow, despite the evidence, he wasn't born in the United States.

During his campaign, the new President had publicly mocked a handicapped reporter, and more recently he agreed to pay twenty-five million dollars to settle a fraud case brought by victims of his Trump University scam.

I called an old Sarasota friend. He had invited me to a party that night. I knew he and his wife had voted for Trump. I was overcome with anxiety. Nauseous.

I told him I couldn't come over and small talk my way through an evening with them and their friends. Even though Hillary Clinton received more than three million more votes, enough people in the nation had decided they would, for the next four years, be led by a reality show host who once pretended to fire Meat Loaf. A liar, caught in a lie, who lies again to explain his earlier lie, and then lies about the lie he told to justify his first lie. The key point: he's a liar. And also now—incredibly—the POTUS.

This lifelong con man, "successful businessman" who'd declared bankruptcy multiple times, on record as an admitted sexual predator, the candidate who'd been enthusiastically supported by both the KKK and the American Nazi Party was now the President of the United States. It was surreal, unimaginable, but there it was.

I knew at that point, I would have to up my medications dramatically to cope with the coming four years. I went back in my files and found an old quote from one of my all-time-favorite writers, Hunter Thompson, during the Nixon years: "The slow-rising central horror of Watergate is not that it might grind down to the reluctant impeachment of a vengeful thug of a President, whose entire political career has been a monument to the same kind of cheap shots and treachery that he finally got nailed for, but that we might somehow fail to learn something from it."

Thompson's slow-rising horror had become a stark reality in little more than forty years.

So I missed the party that night with my friends in Sarasota. That same dynamic, a re-examination of friendships and relationships in the context of that election, has been a hallmark (for me and many of my friends) for the nearly three years since that unfortunate turn in the American *zeitgeist*. It's nightmarish.

People I thought I knew well turned out to share few if any of my values. Or if they did, they sublimated them to cynical considerations: "I need the tax cuts," and "We need to run this country like a business," and "He says exactly what he thinks."

He says what he thinks? So does every four-year-old I've ever met, but I don't want a child running the country!

As the days passed, the grim reality of the election results took hold. The first attempts were made to block entry into the country of Muslims and Latinos and anyone else the new administration wanted me to be afraid of.

I marched, I protested, I used my voice. I joined a support group of friends and actors who met every couple of weeks to remind ourselves that we aren't helpless; things were not in fact spinning out of control.

To our horror, the stories we heard and the interactions we witnessed were increasing: our black, brown, and Jewish friends were being more openly discriminated against in stores and restaurants and on the street. We talked about what we could do to let those folks in our neighborhoods know that we were safe people, they could trust us to help and support them—that we were there to stand up for what was right and fight against what was clearly wrong.

Two members of the group decided that talking wasn't enough and started standing on street corners once a week for a few hours, holding signs to remind passersby THIS IS NOT NORMAL.

Some of my Jewish friends were investigating possible emigration to Israel. Three adopted Syrian children in my neighborhood refused to go to school the day after the election.

Hispanic neighbors were being openly challenged in grocery store checkout lines if they dared speak Spanish to their children and told to "go back where you came from."

Goddammit. The fine, progressive, open-minded city with a long history of Scandinavian openness and compassionate government that I had claimed as my home since 1971 had suddenly morphed into a fearful, suspicious place I almost didn't recognize. Racism and fear of the other are supposed to be unwelcome here.

Hubert Humphrey, a beloved former mayor, US senator, and vice president under Lyndon Johnson, now resting peacefully at Lakewood Cemetery in the middle of the city, made his political bones in the 1940s, firmly championing civil rights. Minnesota was the only state that didn't support the Republican presidential candidate in 1984—Ronald Reagan's second term.

This new landscape was alien to all of us.

A shameful new national governing policy had suddenly appeared and was proclaimed weekly at strangely familiar "rallies" across the country: cruelty for cruelty's sake. This was no longer a question of politics; this new question was one of morality.

If I had been paying closer attention, I might have seen this coming. There were warning signs. Online interactions in the comments sections of most news and political forums revealed a startling number of people who seemed to enjoy mocking liberal sentiments, labeling anyone who expressed concern for the less-fortunate as "snowflakes."

The reality of what was happening to their country seemed not to register with those people in any way.

The facts are right in front of us and on video. Do we ignore them, deny that what we see and hear is real, just create our own reality? The only people I've ever heard use the term "fake news" are Trumpers. They've become like the kid whose mom walks in on him while he's masturbating and he says, "It's not mine. I'm holding it for a friend. I'm not jerking off, that's fake news."

The term "political correctness" was incessantly invoked as a rationale to say and do things previously considered boorish, ignorant, and out of bounds in a civilized world. By sneering and calling anything remotely kind and considerate of another person's beliefs "politically correct," Trump voters basically said, "I reserve my right to be an asshole. Deal with it."

Progressive friends tried in vain to apply facts and reason to what was becoming as all-out assault on truth and verifiable reality. John Cleese of Monty Python fame responded that "Snowflake is a word used by sociopaths in an attempt to discredit the notion of empathy."

George Orwell's classic novel, *1984,* was an oft-quoted source by progressives as the war of fact vs. "alternative fact" picked up steam and filled online threads and coffee shop conversations all over the country.

Trump's favorite line at his Nuremberg-like rallies all over the country had become: "The press is the enemy of the people!" In speaking to a crowd of veterans in July of 2018, Trump actually said, "Don't believe the crap you see from these people, the fake news . . .What you're seeing and what you're reading is not what's happening."

Calling into question objective reality is Rule #1 in the dictator's handbook. Hitler did it. Stalin did it. Mussolini did it. Kim Jong Un and Putin do it. Now a President of the United States was doing it daily. Chilling.

An observation from Thomas Jefferson contained in a letter he wrote to Judge John Tyler in June 1804 seemed to fit the moment perfectly: "No experiment can be more interesting than that which we are now trying, and which we trust will end in establishing the fact that man may be governed by reason and truth. Our first object should therefore be to leave open to him all the avenues to truth, the most effectual heretofore found in the freedom of the press. It is, therefore, the first shut up by those who fear the investigation of their actions."

A warning from 215 years ago from a Hall of Fame Founding Father. Is anybody listening here in 2019?

19

THE MASTER DEBATER

Some years past, entirely before Trump became a national curiosity, I ended a long relationship with a friend I had known since the late eighties. We had an ongoing email discussion that at times produced three or four lengthy exchanges a week.

He was an uncompromising conservative and spent many hours constructing his arguments and presenting them for my consideration in the hope that I would one day surrender and say, "Yes, I have to admit it, you're right and always have been; liberalism is a cancer on the body politic, and Rush Limbaugh is a Deity who Knows All and Must Be Worshipped."

Well, that dog was never going to hunt. Our exchanges continued through the Bush and Obama administrations, reinforced with the occasional in-person conversation whenever he came through town and we had lunch.

Finally in 2012, after more than fifteen years of sometimes funny, sometimes testy personal discussions, one late night around

3:00 a.m., I decided I had spent way too much time patiently poring over his bizarre theories and trying to respond civilly to what I knew to be the purest of pure bullshit. I went back through years of his emails, selecting some of his clearest and most passionately held convictions. Around 5:00 a.m., this is what I wrote:

Old friend,

Let's see if I can boil your political positions, beliefs, and opinions down to a few sentences and sound bites:

Barack Hussein Obama is an incompetent socialist anti-business liar-in-chief and to this point has never accomplished anything important in his life. His middle name is sinister and should always be used when referencing him to point out that he's "not one of us."

There is no such thing as "white privilege" in America.

The fact that 400 people in this country own more combined wealth than the bottom 150 million Americans is a testament to the industry and brains of those 400 people and evidence that over 150 million Americans are lazy and looking for a handout.

Rich people are over-taxed.

Anyone who writes for credible mainstream newspapers or reports on respected networks worldwide are to be labeled "the lame-stream media" and cannot to be trusted. Only right-wing media like *Fox News* present the facts.

Man-made global warming is not a crisis; it is an international conspiracy started by Al Gore for personal, selfish reasons.

Voter fraud is a serious problem in this country, even though no one can find more than a few cases of it happening anywhere.

If you belong to a union, you're a thug.

Of the two Georges, Soros funds socialism in this country, while Bush was an excellent president who was misinformed by others about Iraq's WMDs.

Rush Limbaugh has every right to ridicule the homeless and the poor, even though he makes $400 million a year.

Ann Coulter is a reasonable human being who never makes up shit.

Liberals hate America. On any given subject, liberals don't "get it."

Welfare for the poor is ruining this country, but corporate welfare is a necessary part of doing business in a "free market."

Mitt Romney taking a $77K tax deduction, as "therapy" for a horse, is normal and acceptable; but a poor mother getting $138 in food stamps is "ripping off the taxpayers."

Despite record profits, the oil industry needs those tax subsidies.

A "living wage" is a socialist idea.

Muslims suck; they want to impose Sharia law, and should all be escorted out of this country. Immediately.

Hispanics should be checked on sight for legal status and

escorted out of this country. Immediately. Because they want our jobs.

Affirmative action is unnecessary because there is no racial economic inequality in this country. Affirmative action acts as a racist barrier to white people.

The deficit was never a problem under Bush, but the day Obama was sworn in, it became a huge problem.

Environmentalists are all whacked-out hippies who should be ridiculed and ignored.

Reagan didn't raise taxes eleven times, even though he did.

Reagan didn't trade arms for hostages, even though he did.

Over a hundred people in the Reagan administration weren't indicted, making his administration NOT the most corrupt (officially) administration in history. Even though they were, and his was.

Women are sluts for demanding access to woman-specific healthcare in their insurance plans.

Bill O'Reilly never paid his former producer ten million dollars for her silence on his sexual harassment lawsuit.

Dick Cheney never arranged for his former company to get billions of dollars in no-bid defense contracts during the Iraq War, and Cheney never lied about the reasons he and Bush started it.

Republicans handle money and the economy better than democrats.

If wealthy people pay less in taxes, they'll create more jobs, and that money will trickle down to the rest of us. Even though they did pay less, they didn't create more jobs, and it didn't trickle anywhere but into their offshore bank accounts.

The near total demolition of the economy was caused by democrats who weren't in power, but somehow managed to do it without the republicans' knowledge or power to stop them.

Okay, sorry, that was more than a few.

But over the years, these ideas are just the tip of the iceberg of what I've gleaned from your emails. We've been chatting a long time and I've generally enjoyed it. You've always seemed like a bright man. I don't think you're stupid. Maybe you just have bad luck when thinking.

If this list is even close to summarizing your beliefs, then you have definitely left town on the Crazy Train, and I don't expect you back soon. I really need to know that whoever I'm conversing with is dealing from a clean deck, and I'm convinced you don't even know your deck is dirty.

I would truly like to be able to see things through your eyes, but it takes me too long to unlearn concepts like "respect" and "compassion" and "empathy" and "treating others as you would like to be treated."

Repeating myself in these daily exchanges is getting tiresome, time-consuming, and what's worse, it's keeping me from writing new material for my show. We were better friends when we weren't constantly trying to one-up each other.

It's probably time to agree to disagree and find something—maybe baseball?—we can discuss with less angst and sarcasm. You seem to know almost as much about that as I do, and I actually played the game.

Putting a halt to this frustrating political dialogue would also give me more time to work on my golf. I want to shoot 70 on my 70th birthday next December. I can't do that if I'm spending a lot of time doing this.

Mark

This long-running correspondence ended six years ago, since my friend never wrote back. When I look back on it, I see the genesis of the Trump cult in the formally educated mind of a person I had always thought was a sane human being—until he started sharing his thinking with me. Then it became a weekly series of jaw-dropping moments when the only fitting response seemed to be, "Really? You believe that?"

Another friend of mine once asked me why I bother to respond to Trump voters, or any conservative whose morality and beliefs clash so loudly with mine. I told him that forty years of eating tainted turkey legs at Renaissance festivals most likely impaired my judgment.

I recently designed an approach I now employ when trying to sift through someone's belief systems as I search desperately for common ground—for something, anything that makes sense. It isn't perfect, but it has given me peace, more and better sleep at night, and has dramatically reduced the number of argumentative interactions I now encounter on the internet or in the locker room at the YMCA.

Here's how I do it:

Internet Troll I demand that you thoughtfully consider my position and carefully refute my points, one by one, and then, when I move the goalposts, I'm gonna need you to refute a whole set of new, completely disingenuous points.

Me Somewhere out there is a tree, tirelessly producing oxygen so you can breathe. I think you owe it an apology.

I don't owe such a person a "debate." It's a descent into madness, like listening to a drunk at a sobriety checkpoint insist that he only had one drink. By skipping lightly over the melodrama and moving on to other people who actually have some connection to reality and facts, you give yourself a chance to stay tethered to the truth.

But if one insists on engaging in a pointless exercise, at least try to do it with panache. Here are five approaches you can try that will have little or no effect on your average internet troll, but will leave you feeling satisfied and ready to sleep soundly with a clear conscience when you switch off your bedside IKEA lamp, fluff your pillow, and close your eyes.

1) LOGIC: I see that the chicken nuggets that were on my plate are missing, and my cat is sitting nearby licking his chops. While this does not prove that the cat ate my dinner, it also does not exonerate him.

2) HUMOR: Stop me if you've heard this—a racist, a misogynist, a sexual predator, a pathological liar, a grifter, a con artist, a blackmailer, a money launderer, and a fucking moron walk into a bar. The bartender says, "What'll you have, Mr. President?"

3) COMPASSION: I am overjoyed to learn that the guy who cheated on his first wife with his second, then cheated on her with his third, then cheated on her with a porn star and lied about paying hush money, then said the payments were legal, is finally getting his own day of prayer from the evangelicals.

4) OFFER OF ASSISTANCE: There are two types of Trump supporters: billionaires and idiots. Check your bank account to see which one you might be.

5) PITHY SLOGAN: Impeachment: it's not just for blowjobs any more.

You're welcome.

&

At the height of my frustration with the George W. Bush administration and the entry of the country into the completely unnecessary and brutal Iraq War, I asked our skilled Puke & Snot sketch writer Michael Levin to come up with a political piece that would allow Joe and me a chance to sink our teeth into some more meaningful topical material.

Michael obliged, and that summer we began our annual presentation of The Master Debater, a monument to pure brain-dead politics that we re-write and update and still perform whenever and wherever we find audiences open and ready to laugh at political dumbfuckery in general.

Since the advent of the Dark Times, we've found that audiences have generally been inundated with daily political outrages to the point where we sometimes take pity on them and spare them from yet another reminder that we're living through the most abnormal of days. But when we decide to do the sketch, people invariably go with us and find the laughter as freeing and refreshing as we hope it will always be. That said, here you go, Puke & Snot's current political sketch, presented in print for your enjoyment:

The Master Debater

PUKE I'm going somewhere where the liquor flows freely, the women are fast, and the money rolls in.

SNOT Where would that be?

PUKE   Where else? The government.

SNOT   You? You're going to run for office?

PUKE   I am a new breed of office seeker! In the old days, politicians would pretend to be your friend, only to steal your money, your land, your freedom.

SNOT   And you're different because . . .??

PUKE   I'm not pretending. Let's cut to the chase, people! There's only one reason why I, Ralph Puke, would run for public office—I'm in it for the power! They got it. I want it. I'm going after it.

SNOT   You know it's not that easy to become a leader. You've got to have a campaign. You gotta have ideas, goals, opinions.

PUKE   I told you I was different. I'm a politician with no ideas, no goals, no opinions.

SNOT   What's so different about that?

PUKE   I freely admit it. [TO AUDIENCE] Thank you! Thank you! I'll be freely admitting a lot of things right after they swear me in.

SNOT   Most politicians are careful what they say in public.

PUKE   Yeah, well most politicians give a damn about what the public thinks. I can't be bothered with public opinion. The public is stupid.

SNOT   Really? What about these people here?

PUKE   [PAUSE] Oh . . . oh no, these people are smart and

perceptive. I'm talking about the OTHER public. [TO AUDIENCE] Thank god, they're not here, we can talk freely.

SNOT   Who do you think you're fooling? These people won't be blinded by a smooth talker with a cheesy smile. You've got to have more than that.

PUKE   I've also got sparkly eyes.

SNOT   What about your issues?

PUKE   My issues? Well, there's my drinking. That's ALWAYS been an issue.

SNOT   That's not important!

PUKE   Maybe not to you, but I've got a dozen bartenders and their families depending on me.

SNOT   I'm talking about issues that affect the lives of your constituents.

PUKE   My what?

SNOT   Your constituents. If you're elected, you're going to have constituents.

PUKE   I'll take Metamucil.

SNOT   People take these things very seriously. Are you prepared to debate other candidates?

PUKE   I'll debate anyone, anywhere, anytime!

SNOT   You're good at debating?

PUKE   Sir, I'm a master debater.

SNOT   I've heard that about you. You've been doing it for a while, I'll bet.

PUKE   Off and on. Off and on. Ever since high school.

SNOT   Were you on the team?

PUKE   No, alone mostly.

SNOT   Okay, let's get started.

PUKE   What?

SNOT   [QUICKLY] With your campaign, your campaign! Let's pretend I'm a member of the press.

PUKE   Is this a temporary position?

SNOT   Yes, why?

PUKE   From the looks of your shirt, I can see you're not PERMANENT press. [PAUSE FOR GROAN] See, I've gotta find a different line of work. I just don't know what's funny anymore.

SNOT   Don't start trouble. Can you do this?

PUKE   Do what?

SNOT   Take questions from the audience. They need to know where you stand. They need to see if you can hold up under the pressure. [HE MOVES OUT INTO THE AUDIENCE]

PUKE   Of course. I'll take five questions during this press conference.

SNOT   [FROM AISLE] How many?

PUKE   Four now.

SNOT   Okay, Mister Candidate?

PUKE   Yes, the journalist in the tights.

SNOT   Can you prove you're a citizen of this country?

PUKE   Yes, I can. I'm working three jobs, I have no money, and my home is in foreclosure.

SNOT   Good enough. [HE HAS MOVED TO ANOTHER SPOT] Mr. Candidate?

PUKE   Yes, the large reporter with the drinking problem.

SNOT   Thank you. What political party do you belong to?

PUKE   I represent the party of family values and fiscal responsibility.

SNOT   How many times have you been married?

PUKE   Three.

SNOT   Had any bankruptcies?

PUKE   Only six. What's your point?

SNOT   Never mind. Sir! Sir! I have a question! [HE'S MOVED AGAIN]

PUKE   Yes, you, the strangely familiar journalist in the red shirt.

SNOT   Thank you. People like to know their leaders are well-informed. What do you read?

PUKE   Read?

SNOT   Yes. What newspapers, books, magazines—what do you read?

PUKE   Well . . . I read *Catcher in the Rye*.

SNOT   Really? You read *Catcher in the Rye*?

PUKE   I certainly did.

SNOT   What was your favorite part.

PUKE   [PAUSE] When he caught all that rye. I also read a book on anti-gravity.

SNOT   Really? Was it good?

PUKE   Yes. I couldn't put it down. But my favorite book is the Bible.

SNOT   I find that hard to believe. What's your favorite chapter?

PUKE   Chapter 11.

SNOT   That's what I thought. Along those lines, a follow-up question. What will you do about the education gap?

PUKE   Nothing, I love the poorly educated.

SNOT   You do?

PUKE   Of course. How do you think I'm planning on getting elected?

SNOT   On the remote possibility that could happen, what's the first thing you'll do when you're elected?

PUKE   I'll ask for a recount.

SNOT   Right. [MOVED AGAIN] A question over here!

PUKE   You with the spinach in your teeth, go ahead.

SNOT   Thank you.

SNOT   What would you say to people who call you dangerous and bigoted?

PUKE   I would ask them to stop quoting me accurately.

SNOT   Okay, where do you stand on the homeless?

PUKE   Usually I just try to step over them.

SNOT   What are you going to do about the long lines of jobless people in the inner cities?

PUKE   I'm going to move the unemployment offices to the suburbs.

SNOT   What should we do with people who rely on government handouts but are too lazy to work?

PUKE   They should be kicked out of Congress.

SNOT   A question about crime: what should we do about repeat offenders?

PUKE   Quit re-electing them.

SNOT   Okay, another question about crime. What will you do about crime in the streets?

PUKE   I'm gonna reduce crime in the streets by 50 percent.

SNOT   How are you gonna do that?

PUKE   I'm gonna build more streets.

SNOT   Will you build a wall on the border?

PUKE   Absolutely. I don't think any Americans should be allowed to escape my policies.

SNOT   All right, let's shift gears to social issues. What's your opinion on marriage equality?

PUKE   I support it. I believe that suffering should be universal.

SNOT   So it doesn't bother you when you see two men holding hands?

PUKE   Of course not. That just means there are two more women for me to strike out with. Next question.

SNOT   Have you ever smoked marijuana?

PUKE   Yes I did, but I quit.

SNOT   Why?

PUKE   It interfered with my drinking.

SNOT   What about the war on terror?

PUKE   I'm still fighting the war on drugs.

SNOT   *Aha!* So you're not concerned about terror.

PUKE   I'm terrified I'll run out of drugs.

SNOT   Don't you realize that there are religious fanatics out there who are out to destroy this country?

PUKE   I thought the Mormons were peaceful.

SNOT   Not the Mormons, you idiot! Are you largely clueless?

PUKE   I try to be, but my staff keeps giving me these damn memos. [PAUSE] See, as long as I've got two or three people laughing at it, I'm gonna do that joke. That's my FEMA joke.

SNOT   What's a FEMA joke?

PUKE   The rest of them will get it in 5–7 weeks. [TO AUDIENCE] Okay, you got me. I am a resolute and fearless leader, but I don't read anything, I can barely put two thoughts together on any subject, and yes, I am clueless.

SNOT   Then what are you qualified for?

PUKE   Jury duty?

SNOT   Okay, one last question. What about a woman's right to choose?

PUKE   I'm against that.

SNOT   Why?

PUKE   Take a look at some of the bozos these women have chosen. You tell me.

SNOT   I'm talking about having babies!

PUKE   If I can stop this knucklehead from reproducing, I've done more than most.

SNOT   I wouldn't vote for you if you were running unopposed!

PUKE   If I was running unopposed, you wouldn't HAVE to vote for me. [TO AUDIENCE] Are we going too fast?

SNOT   You have no background, you have no experience, you have no intelligence. What makes you think you could hold public office?

PUKE   If you have a background, the press will mangle it. If you have experience, you're already disillusioned. And if you had any intelligence, you wouldn't be running for office in the first place.

SNOT   You know what the truly frightening thing is?

PUKE   What?

SNOT   You're starting to make sense.

PUKE   I told you. I'm a natural. I've come to the sad realization that any yahoo can win an election if he's got a good publicist.

SNOT   Well, allow me to assume that position.

PUKE   Not so fast. Once I'm in office and you're just another taxpayer, THEN you can "assume the position."

SNOT No, I'm saying you should allow me to be your campaign manager.

PUKE Do you have any experience?

SNOT None whatsoever.

PUKE Perfect. You're just the man for the job. I'll make you head of Homeland Security. [THEY SHAKE HANDS] Snottie, yer doin' a heckuva job.

SNOT Thank you. Now first of all, you're gonna need a slogan.

PUKE A what?

SNOT A catchy phrase that will endear you to the hearts and minds of the voting public.

PUKE Of course. I got it. [TO AUDIENCE] "There once was a man from Nantucket…"

SNOT Not THAT catchy. It should say something about you as a person.

PUKE How about this: "I don't need a wax job, I'm smooth enough for you."

SNOT You're gonna need a belt sander. Try another one.

PUKE How about this? "It's morning in my tights."

SNOT And I can see the dark side of the moon. Try again.

PUKE Okay—here's a winner: Vote for Puke: Stop Electile Dysfunction!

SNOT That's it! A noble sentiment. Who could argue with that? I like it! Okay, get out there and start kissing some babies.

PUKE   What?

SNOT   You're running for office, they expect it, start kissing babies.

PUKE   They expect it? Cool . . .[TO WOMAN IN AUDIENCE] Hey baby . .

SNOT   Get back here, you couldn't run for a bus. You can't go around kissing strangers.

PUKE   Hey, it kept me out of the army. I know one thing—if a campaign lasts more than four hours, consult your doctor immediately.

SNOT   This political stuff is bombing, let's get out of here.

PUKE   We can't get out of here; we don't have an exit strategy. [TO AUDIENCE] Oh, did we go too far?

Just a random collection of jokes about a politician who is thunderously incompetent, always says the wrong thing, doesn't read, has no historical knowledge, lies easily and often, is truthful only accidentally and hilariously, and in normal times would be a horrible candidate. This is familiar territory for all of us by now.

Good comic actors long before Charlie Chaplin did *The Great Dictator* understood that satire was a weapon that can be used to enlighten as well as entertain. Mort Sahl, one of my favorite political comedians from the sixties, said, "Comedians have to challenge the power. Comedians should be dangerous and devastating—and funny. That's the hardest part."

The king's jester was allowed to speak truth to power without fearing for his life. The king wrote it off to insanity, but the people knew the jester was right. The late George Carlin is my personal political comic hero, I saw him perform live at a Minnesota college early in his career, and despite being high and smoking a joint throughout his performance, he was brilliant. I think. I was stoned at the time.

Carlin's long, consistently sharp and uncompromising career was spent speaking truth to power. Among the current crop of comic actors who make me laugh and think and applaud are Jon Stewart, Stephen Colbert, Samantha Bee, and Seth Myers.

Colbert's appearance at the Washington Press Corps dinner with President George W. Bush sitting six feet away was one of the finest, ballsiest moments in the history of Court Jester vs. the King. Jim Jefferies is a stand-up comic whose take on gun control is one of the funniest and most pointed you'll ever see. He makes it work not only because his observations about the usual excuses for Second Amendment abuses are so transparently ridiculous, but because he's an Australian who can look at American gun culture as an outsider.

In the end, laughing at the incompetence, ignorance, and arrogance of the people who somehow end up in positions of great power and responsibility in our lives may be the only way for us to keep some semblance of our sanity. Someday we're going to look back at decisions all of us made in this Trump moment about what America should have been and what America could have been.

No one should be taking any cues from Donald Trump. He's polluted the public dialogue, he's debased our military and our fellow Americans and attacked our institutions. His cruelty toward immigrants and poor people seeking only what our ancestors sought—a place to live and work and raise their children free from fear and hardship—has become the defining theme of his presidency. He has turned the welcoming words on the Statue of Liberty into a sick joke.

Where he steps, weeds die. If no one is willing to turn him out of office using the levers of power provided by the Constitution, maybe he can be laughed out.

Democracy is not a spectator sport. It requires participation by the people for it to survive. Politics is a subject in this country that divides families, starts bar fights, breaks up marriages, causes million-man and women's marches, and occupies much of our mental energy. But in the end, democracy demands everyone's involvement.

If you're not "interested" in politics, you can be sure that the people who loan you money, decide your interest rates, zone your neighborhoods, fund your schools, set your tax rates, send your kids to war, legislate your healthcare, decide your retirements, and determine your wage scales are not only interested in politics, they're *involved* in politics. If you're going to simply give them that power over your life without your input, they will welcome it. And you will have to take your chances that they will act in your best interests. Good luck with that.

I love that my job sometimes allows me to become a court jester of old and tell the king that he's naked when everyone else is pretending he's fully clothed.

20

FOR THE CONNOISSEURS

When you do something you love for over forty years, you begin to notice that the people you did it with—shared the stages, programs, stories, and audiences with—start quietly making their exits. As in departing. As in no curtain calls, no encores. It's a bit startling, something we try to treat with acceptance and casual good humor in the show. But the cold shower of reality you take when the ones closest to you have to say goodbye is always unwelcome, never easy.

Much of the time I spent on stages large and small since that first knee-knocking appearance in *January Thaw* in high school has been outdoors in the sun and the rain and the wind at Renaissance festivals across the country. And lately, some of the important original movers and shakers of that odd little corner of the entertainment universe have taken reluctant early retirement.

The Renaissance festival community I've been a part of since

1974 recently lost one of its long-standing and most-loved members, the legendary Johnny Fox. He departed, as the good ones often do, much too soon, and the gigantic hole he left in our little space time continuum will never be filled with a spirit as memorable, as generous, or as talented.

Johnny was a friend of mine and Joe's since our early days working the Colorado Renaissance Festival in the 1980s. He asked us to join him at the Boulder Mall for Friday night performances in puffy shirts and jeans that always gave us a good hat-passing start to the festival weekend and provided plenty of food and beer money for us and our friends. Johnny was loved by all, and that's not hyperbole.

He would stay onstage as long as it took after every show, signing autographs, talking to the kids, taking pictures. His passion for the old circus traditions and the people who created them was palpable. He seemed to know all the old side-show performers from every American circus. His sword-swallowing show was the best on the circuit, mostly because he never took it so seriously that the audience ever thought he was trying to impress them.

He did amazing close-up magic, startling feats of sword-and-dagger-swallowing, and did it all while making you laugh hard enough to come back the following season to get that experience again with your kids. I was humbled to be asked to speak at the celebration of Johnny's life, and this is what I said:

The Fantastic Mr. Fox. A good movie. And a great man. I'm truly honored to be able to say a few words in public about a guy who touched so many lives in the too-short time he was with us. I'll share a few fun memories, the kind I know Johnny would love to hear me talk about. I'm just going to go ahead and assume he's in the back of the hall right now, ready to be entertained.

There's a thing psychotherapists call "euphoric recall." I'd rather not tell you how I learned that term; you'll just have to trust me here. But euphoric recall is a psychological term for the tendency of people to remember past experiences in a positive light, while overlooking the negatives associated with that event. With people, it becomes difficult to remember any unpleasant things about someone right after they move out of our lives. We tend to remember only the good stuff. My guess is with Johnny, it'll be all euphoric, all the time, for a long, long time. I'll tell you why.

Johnny was at the roast they threw for John Gamoke and me late in the summer four years ago after we had announced it would be our final year at the Colorado festival. After everyone had their fun roasting us, it was our turn. John and I took the mic and went around the room and nailed everyone who was there without mercy. I had just finished with [our longtime friend] Arsene by saying, "And then there's Arsene. Like we need another reason to hate the French. He works silently and the audience responds the same way."

I got a good laugh with that one. Then here's what I said when I looked over at Johnny: "And there's Johnny Fox. I've been watching your show for twenty-five years, it's all about torture. Eye-gouging, nails pounded in your head, a spike through your tongue. If you're so into showing us torture, you should do a show about people WATCHING your show. Just answer one question, Fox: for an act that has so many sharp objects, how can it be so amazingly dull?"

I spent a lot of time preparing for that roast. I thought those jokes were pretty good. Johnny was laughing hard, but he was the only one. The rest of the room was just staring at me. It occurred to me instantly that I was going after the one person in the room that everyone really liked. There was nothing about Johnny that was evenly *remotely* annoying. It was like roasting Pope Francis.

I stopped and moved on to easier targets.

I ran into Johnny the first time at the Ringling Medieval Faire in the early eighties in Sarasota. It was one of his favorite Renaissance shows, not only because it was staged on the 66-acre grounds of one of America's most famous circus owners, but it was only an hour from Tampa where a lot of the old retired circus sideshow guys lived. And Johnny knew most of them.

We did that festival for some years, and Johnny always thought John Ringling would have loved it. He definitely would have watched Johnny's show, and back then he certainly would have hired him.

Johnny asked Joe and me to stop backstage one afternoon at the Ringling show. He wanted us to meet a friend of his named

Melvin Burkhardt. Melvin was in his eighties, and Johnny had invited Melvin to come down from Tampa. He was excited to see him, and he introduced him to Joe and me as the guy who invented the "blockhead" bit where he nailed a spike into his head.

As we were talking with Melvin, he reached into his pocket and pulled out a small jackknife and said, "Let me show you something." For the next few minutes, he dazzled us with some incredible close-up magic—flipping the jackknife over and over and seemingly changing its colors every time he did. He did similar tricks with a set of dice, changing the numbers as we watched.

When Melvin was finished entertaining me and Joe, Johnny invited him to go out onstage and do ten minutes of his old sideshow routine. Joe and I walked around to the front and watched. As soon as Melvin hit the stage, the years dropped away. It was as if he was a thirty-year-old performer back on the sideshow circuit again. His rap was as quick and fresh as it must have been when he was doing it for Ringling. Johnny watched him work and led the applause when he finished, then he introduced him to the crowd. Melvin got a standing ovation. (Partly because the producer hadn't provided enough benches, but still, a standing ovation.)

That was Johnny doing the kind of thing Johnny was famous for—sharing the spotlight. He loved the guys who pioneered the routines he practiced. He sought them out and honored them. And they loved him for it. He seemed to know everybody, and everybody knew him.

I was back in Sarasota about ten years ago walking around St. Armand's Circle on Lido Key on a Sunday. St. Armand's is a circular park built by John Ringling as a place for his circus band to perform concerts on Sundays for the Sarasota folks. They use it for all sorts of events now: art shows, band concerts, festivals.

This particular Sunday they had a stage set up with about fifty chairs for the audience. There was a thing going on, lots of well-dressed people, some in circus costumes. I stopped to check it out.

Turned out it was the Annual Ring of Fame Awards celebrating circus greats down the years. There are bronze plates in the concrete all around the park. They were announcing the inductees.

So I watched. The second name they announced was a guy they called the World's Greatest Sword Swallower.

He was an older guy with red hair, Red Stuart. He went up, accepted the award, spoke briefly and sat down. I worked my way over to where he was sitting at the end of the row.

During a break in the ceremony, I introduced myself and I asked him if he knew Johnny Fox.

Red looked around and said, "Of course, is he here?"

I said, "No, he's just a friend of mine."

"Well, tell him I said hi."

"I will," I said. Everybody knew Johnny.

Johnny, Arsene, and Joe, and I worked together a lot back in the eighties and nineties. We put together a show for a two-week run at Minneapolis's biggest comedy club and called it *The Knights of Pythias Circle of Death Family Fun Show*. Arsene opened, Johnny did the middle thirty minutes, and Joe and I anchored it. We were always aware we had to be really on top of it because those two guys had pretty much sucked all the air out of the room by the time we took the stage.

Then we all worked together at Disney World one summer, doing three outdoor shows a night for the Mouse. We shared a condo because I knew how much fun it would be listening to Johnny and Arsene argue all night about who came up with the cigarette bit first and who had the right to use it onstage the next day.

After the show, we'd go into Orlando to a place we could shoot pool. Johnny would take a cue from the wall, unscrew the two halves, swallow the smaller half, pull it out and say, "Yeah, this one's about right."

While people were gaping at Johnny, Arsene would pick up four pool balls and start juggling them over the table. Later on, we'd find a restaurant and Johnny would do his classic eye-gouge trick with a waitress and totally freak her out. Joe and I were simple bystanders. We couldn't compete at that level.

Joe and I had only been doing the Colorado festival for a few years, but Johnny and I had already had quite a few conversations about the festival circuit, and I knew there was one thing that really bothered him and something he had no patience for—other acts stealing his material. Or anyone's material. That made him mad.

And rightfully so, an artist's tricks, jokes, patter, are his bread and butter.

But there are acts out there who don't care about that little detail. So one Saturday afternoon, Johnny knocked on my trailer door and said, "I might get fired, I just took care of some business, and the guy's heading to the office to tell them what happened. He's bleeding a little."

"What happened?"

He said, "You know that new magician they hired who's been doing my stuff?" (I had heard about him.)

"I'm pretty sure he's also been doing some of Puke & Snot's best lines too."

"Really?"

Johnny said, "Yeah, so I just went over to his stage and told him to knock that crap off and quit doing other people's shows, and he said, 'I can do any material I want, you don't own those tricks or those jokes.' He was right in my face, and I was holding my bag of coins, my tips from the last show, and I just reacted and cold-cocked him with the bag—opened up a cut over his eye. He went down like a tree. I could be in trouble."

I asked, "You sure he was doing our stuff too?"

Johnny said, "Yeah, he was doing your pirate joke."

"Can I borrow your bag of coins?"

We had a long talk about the bleeding magician. We decided Johnny did what he needed to do.

In the end it turned out okay—the guy healed up. He didn't last long at the festival. Everybody thought he got what he deserved. Everybody knew Johnny, and that was it.

The Bleeding Magician became a footnote in Renfest history. And that's about as anonymous and unknown as you can get.

There's one show I'll never forget, and I'll wrap this up. Johnny and Arsene put together a show in Colorado one summer called *Fox and The Mahatma*. They combined their talents once a day in a show where Johnny played the straight man and Arsene came out from backstage in a gigantic turban smoking a cigarette and holding a bag of booze. The show was a two-man routine where Johnny would ask Arsene to help him do a trick, they'd totally screw it up, Arsene would accidentally set something on fire, and props would get dropped and destroyed. Johnny played the patient straight man to Arsene's fool. It was brilliant.

I've been around festival shows more than forty years. I've seen The Flying Karamazovs, Rogue Oaf and Fool, Avner the Eccentric, The Flaming Idiots, Penn and Teller, all the classics—and I can honestly say that none of them made me laugh harder and longer than *Fox and The Mahatma*. It was a show they did, as Johnny would say, "for the connoisseurs." And many in the cast showed up to see it.

Johnny let Arsene have a lot of the laughs, or maybe Arsene insisted, I don't know. But Johnny was one of the best straight men I've ever seen in that half-hour show. It could have headlined anywhere in the country.

Johnny's leaving has affected all of us in ways we have yet to know. I won't be getting any more late-night phone calls with newly discovered dietary advice. As I got older, Johnny was concerned with what he could do to make sure I had a long, productive life. Since I'm from Minnesota, he knew I was addicted to Tater Tot hotdish, and he was sure it was going to eventually kill me.

I won't be getting that knock on my trailer door after a festival day that would precede an hour of really cool stories about people and places I didn't know and probably would never experience; no more calls from Mexico in the middle of the winter telling me to get down there to join him, that he was working some gigs and had a place for me to stay.

No more of those backstage discussions about what makes something funny. Arsene and Johnny would talk about tricks and illusions, Johnny and I would talk about comedy and why stuff was funny.

I used to tell him to drop the "septic" bit. I told him it didn't connect to anything else in the show and wasn't funny. He liked the line, "There will always be septics—er, skeptics, there will always be skeptics." I think he finally did stop using it.

He'd also tell me if he thought something John and I were doing wasn't working. I'd just look at him and say, "There will always be septics."

I loved his Shih-Tzu joke. After he'd swallow the balloon,

he'd ask the kids what their favorite animal was: "I can do a Shih-Tzu." Always made me laugh. But that's because Shih-Tzu is a funny word. Like schnauzer. I can do five schnauzer jokes right now, and every one of them is funny. And not one of them is appropriate in this setting. Johnny finally stopped doing the Shih-Tzu joke, I think because of the kids. He didn't want to do any material that the parents would have to explain to the kids in the car on the way home.

I, on the other hand, literally designed my show around that concept. That's the difference between a performer who actually thinks about the impact his show has on his audience, and me.

When my two sons were much younger, they learned some very cool sleight-of-hand tricks from the Fantastic Mr. Fox. He always took time for kids at shows. And the kids always came back every year till they had kids of their own, and even until their kids had kids.

What a legacy he left. The Fantastic Mr. Fox. Real magic exists. Stay fiercely optimistic.

The Fantastic Mr. Fox at the Annapolis Boat Show, October 2015

❧

LASTLY

The acting profession is filled with classic examples of the old saying, "When God closes a door, he opens a window." My smartypants self would add "because God farts. A lot."

Many windows were opened for me since I first decided to write a little comedy show and perform it outdoors with an equally naïve and crazy friend and fellow Twin Citian, Joe Kudla. We had an idea that fit a certain time and emerging phenomenon, the seventies and Renaissance festivals. We were actors, we liked dressing up like a couple of bizarre Monty Python knockoffs and making people laugh, and Minnesotans enjoyed driving twenty miles west of Minneapolis in the early fall to spend a few hours watching jugglers, sword swallowers, magicians, ropewalkers, mimes, jousts with wooden lances, and clowns of all kinds, us among them.

Over the years, we kept the show moving forward, finding new audiences all over North America. When Joe, the amazing and original Snot, died suddenly in 2008, our old friend John Gamoke stepped in. In one week he was able to walk out onstage, make it his own, and get a standing ovation.

In the fall of 2017, when John decided ten years was enough, Scott Jorgenson took the mantle and the show moved into its forty-fourth year without missing a beat. These enormously talented men figured out immediately how to handle the rain, the heat, the noise, the wind, and the alcohol-infused heckler, and make the laughter loud and long enough to bring people back for more.

The Original Snot, Joe Kudla

It's been eleven years since the original Snot, Joe Kudla, took "early retirement." It's remarkable the number of people who continue to tell me every festival day how much they miss his presence on the planet. The ingenious comedy work he did over thirty-four years still inspires applause and happy crowds.

Thomas Snot, Jr/John Paul Gamoke

Once in a while I pop in a DVD or I'll click on a YouTube sketch from those days and, without fail, I laugh out loud watching the original Snot do his thing, truly one of the funniest physical actors I ever met or had the honor to share a stage with. He left a large empty space when he stepped out of the canoe.

The show got lucky when John agreed to step in, and now Scott is continuing the madness. John and Scott are uniquely their own Snots. They bring the laughs, and audiences are still getting their money's worth. For the ten years John did the show, someone would invariably walk up to John and tell him he had big shoes to fill. John would always respond with "Not to mention pants." Perfect.

AREA MAN TAKES MAJOR STEP TO RECLAIM HIS DIGNITY

After ten years appearing as Thomas Snot Jr at Renaissance festivals from Maryland to Florida to Colorado to Minnesota, area-man John Paul Gamoke recently announced his intention to "never be seen in those goddam tights again." Reaction from friends and neighbors has been universally positive.

Henry Hammerschmidt, Mr. Gamoke's longtime neighbor, said, "We've been waiting for him to regain his senses—he seems like he's almost back to normal now. That was a weird time in his life, and we're all glad it's over. Now we can enjoy poker games in John's kitchen again without the uncomfortable silences whenever someone asked him about his next gig."

In a recent interview in his suburban backyard where we found him re-sodding some bare spots on his lawn and setting rabbit traps, Gamoke said, "I don't know what happened—guess I thought doing bad comedy outdoors in the rain with a stupid British accent was somehow a step up in my career. I blame it on my wife. She could have stopped me anytime, but I think she enjoyed watching me humiliate myself."

Gamoke's two adult children say they're relieved and happy. Both plan on coming home for Thanksgiving this year for the first time since Mr. Gamoke began his bizarre avocation.

Mr. Gamoke has enrolled in a recovery program for Renaissance performers, has started a GoFundMe site to help with the financial burden, and by all accounts is making good progress.

"I still slip every now and then, but I'm getting better at normal human interaction. Yesterday I asked a stock boy at Cub Foods where I could find a henway. When he said, 'What's a henway?,' I couldn't stop myself: 'About three pounds.' He hit me in the face with a cantaloupe. But I deserved it and I won't press charges. It's a day-at-a-time thing for me, like everyone else who's faced these life challenges."

His longtime comedy partner refused to be interviewed for this article, but did say that he was surprised Mr. Gamoke lasted as long as he did, and surmised that without the daily pint of Maker's Mark before every show, Gamoke likely would have quit after the first season. There will be a private ceremony in December where Mr. Gamoke's tights, his puffy shirts, and his costume boots will be burned. The public is not invited.

Scott Snot, Version 3.0/Scott Jorgenson

Scott Jorgenson actually had a life before he decided to ruin it by becoming an actor. He managed a private practice as an optician for eighteen years, so it takes on a whole new meaning when he does the "I'd Like To Buy An Eye" pirate sketch.

If you saw him in his first television commercial for Arctic Cat where he wore nothing but a Speedo, you may still not have fully recovered. That was an astonishingly brave thing to do.

Taking on the Puke & Snot Show as Scott Snot is child's play in comparison.

Scott has appeared in over thirty television spots and 350 radio spots, selling you everything from snowmobiles to cereal. He's also popped up on some of the Twin Cities most popular stages. He is a featured actor on some of the funniest YouTube videos ever produced. Ask him about *Shepherd Hunting* and *Fear of Girls*. John Gamoke's Snot has a worthy heir. The proof went on display at the Minnesota Renaissance Festival in Shakopee in summer 2018.

❧

There are a thousand ways to make your way onto a stage, and I've been lucky enough to find more than a few that paid me to do it. Stages come in many forms, a theater, a video studio, a movie set, a street corner, a teacher's lectern, Upper Duff's, a circus sideshow, a karaoke bar, a pulpit, a woodsy lane, or a decrepit pirate ship at a Renaissance festival.

If you're so inclined and are willing to spend a lot of your offstage time saying things like, "You want to supersize that?," get out there, find a stage, and scratch that itch.

I read about an actor in Chicago, Mike Nussbaum. As of 2019, he's playing the Gravedigger in a Chicago Shakespeare Theater's production of *Hamlet*.

At ninety-five, Mike Nussbaum is the oldest working actor in the 50,000-member Actors' Equity Association. His resume goes back eighty years, with roles in the original *American Buffalo* and *Glengarry Glen Ross* on Broadway as notable highlights. He was in *Field of Dreams, Men in Black,* and *Fatal Attraction.*

David Mamet was asked about Mike recently, and he responded in typical Mamet fashion, "It's wonderful to work with Mike because, like any artist, like any actor, he's just unusual. You're constantly saying, 'My God, where did that come from?' It's not coming out of a bag of 'acting moments.' That's all bullshit. It's coming out of— who the hell knows where? You either got it or you don't, and Mike certainly does."

Nussbaum talks about eating right and exercising as important factors in his longevity on stage. But he also says, "I'm lucky, it's just pure luck. This is fun. And for an old man to have fun is unusual."

I know what you mean, Mike. I know what you mean. There are many days when I'd rather be lucky than good. You, of course, are both. Let's get together and do *King Lear*. I'd have fun just standing in the wings, holding your cloak, watching you work.

ABOUT THE AUTHOR

Mark Sieve is an actor, producer, director, and with this second book, possibly a writer. His writing career was foreshadowed in 1956 when, as an eighth grade student at St. Mary's Elementary in Ellsworth, Minnesota, he won the Nobles County Spelling Bee and advanced to the state contest in Minneapolis, where he was promptly crushed by the city kids with larger vocabularies and bigger dictionaries.

There's your champ on the right.

His 2009 award-winning first book, *Call Me Puke: A Life on the Dirt Circuit*, and has sold more than 6,000 copies. Not bad for an exercise in self-promotion.

Disturbance in the Farce: Puke—The Final Chapter, Volume 1 is the second in a series describing the life stories of a small-town Minnesota kid whose remarkable good fortune through a lifetime of fellowship, family, and friendship allowed him to stand many times in the spotlight and accept the applause for performances that were largely attributable to others more deserving; parents who loved their son enough to let him find his way; teachers, students, a patient wife, and two talented sons; actors, mentors, four brothers and a sister, coaches who cared, directors who trusted, and audiences at Renaissance festivals who kept coming back for more.

All of them made the journey a walk in the park. And it looks like it's gonna be a gorgeous sunset.

CALL ME PUKE
A Life on the Dirt Circuit

Mark Sieve's first book, *Call Me Puke: A Life on the Dirt Circuit*, published in 2009, won a Midwest Book Award for Humor.

"To someone like me, who had come up in magic with the idea that the tricks and visual effects were the show and the performer was just the delivery system, Puke & Snot were startling. Their show wasn't about what they did. It was about what they were."
—from the Foreword by Teller, the silent creepy half of
Penn & Teller

"The most successful act on the Renaissance festival circuit, the nonpareils, Puke & Snot."   —Calvin Trillin, *The New Yorker*

"The book lives up to its brilliant title. As a quintessential insider, Sieve dissects the underbelly of Renaissance festivals with swashbuckling aplomb and rapier wit. His portrayals of the eclectic coveys of performers evoke a hot dusty *American Idol*. Except EVERYONE has a British accent. From the sublime, to the ridiculous, to the certifiably insane, it's a strange but fascinating way to make a buck."
—Patrick O'Brien, actor, stage/movies/television

"Does the Disney Company owe its entertainment renaissance to Puke & Snot? Let's just say they were the canaries in the coal mine."   —From After the Foreword by Stephen Hedrick
former producer, Disney Creative, Orlando

"I loved this book! Mark is a wonderful writer and storyteller. I found it fascinating, charming, insightful, touching and . . . oh yeah, absolutely hilarious! I loved the stories of the wacky early years of the Renaissance festivals and how the wonderful comedy duo of Puke & Snot came to be. But Mark also lets us in on where he came from and what inspired him, from baseball to teaching to acting to tights. And his tribute to his partner Joe is both delightful and very moving. A great great read!"
—Sue Scott, actor/comedian, *A Prairie Home Companion*

Made in the USA
Columbia, SC
09 August 2019